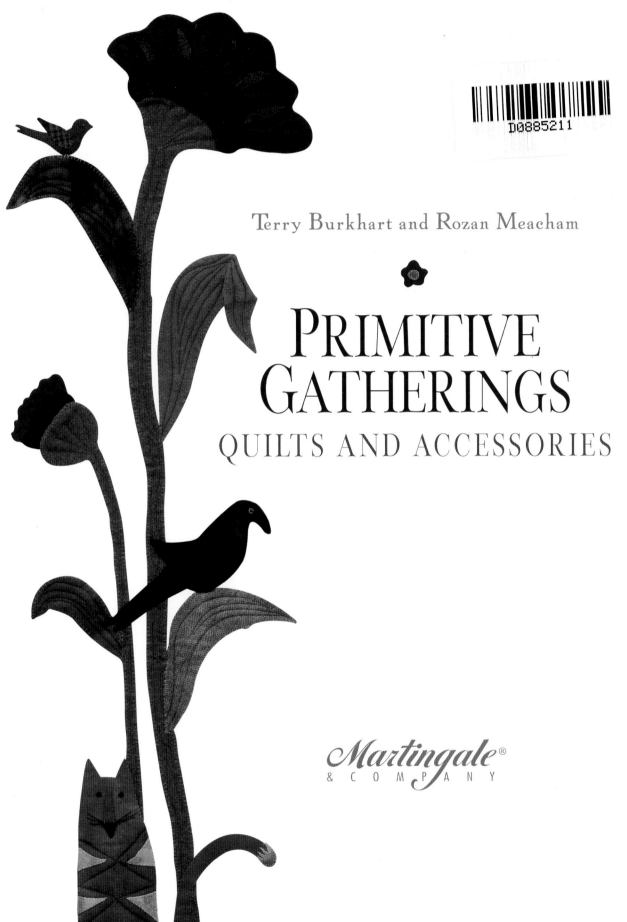

Terry Burkhart and Rozan Meacham

PRIMITIVE GATHERINGS
QUILTS AND ACCESSORIES

Martingale®
& COMPANY

That Patchwork Place® is an imprint of Martingale & Company®.

Primitive Gatherings: Quilts and Accessories
© 2006 by Terry Burkhart and Rozan Meacham

Martingale & Company
20205 144th Avenue NE
Woodinville, WA 98072-8478 USA
www.martingale-pub.com

Printed in China
11 10 09 08 07 06   8 7 6 5 4 3 2 1

Mission Statement

Dedicated to providing quality products and service to inspire creativity.

Library of Congress Cataloging-in-Publication Data
Burkhart, Terry.
    Primitive gatherings : quilts and accessories / Terry Burkhart and Rozan Meacham.
        p. cm.
    ISBN 1-56477-650-6
    1. Quilting—Patterns. 2. Needlework—Patterns. 3. Decoration and ornament, Rustic. I. Meacham, Rozan. II. Title.
    TT835.B843 2006
    746.46—dc22

                                                                                2005028412

Credits

President • *Nancy J. Martin*
CEO • *Daniel J. Martin*
VP and General Manager • *Tom Wierzbicki*
Publisher • *Jane Hamada*
Editorial Director • *Mary V. Green*
Managing Editor • *Tina Cook*
Technical Editor • *Ellen Pahl*

Copy Editor • *Ellen Balstad*
Design Director • *Stan Green*
Illustrator • *Laurel Strand*
Cover and Text Designer • *Trina Craig*
Studio Photographer • *Brent Kane*
Location Photographer • *John Hamel*
Photography Stylist • *Ellen Pahl*

Dedication

To Terry's daughter Anne Guizzo, for patiently assisting in the writing, sketching, and compilation of the manuscript. We appreciate all the time you sacrificed. Without you, this book would still be a stack of papers on the kitchen table.

Acknowledgments

Special thanks to the editors and staff at Martingale & Company for all the help, and answers to endless questions. They were kind enough to hold our hands as we muddled through the process of writing this book.

We extend a heartfelt thank you to our Bible study group for giving us support and helpful advice.

Sarah Achterhof and MaryLynn Konyu were a wonderful help in assisting Rozan through all of the ups and downs.

Martha Dirks, MaryLynn Konyu, and Amy Smith contributed their incredible skills to the workmanship of these quilts; the quilts will be enjoyed by all and are greatly appreciated by us.

Retta Warehime was the driving force in starting this book. Thanks for the extra push.

We greatly appreciate all the girls at Pieceable Dry Goods. You have been supportive beyond friendship.

And to our husbands, Keith Burkhart and Pat Meacham, we want to express our gratitude for waiting through this never-ending project. You both provided a tremendous amount of support and encouragement.

CONTENTS

INTRODUCTION · 4

PROJECTS

Primitive Gatherings Quilt · 5

Colors of Autumn Table Runner · 24

Antique Pull Toy Rug · 29

Rules for Country Living
Wall Hanging · 33

Country Homecoming Quilt · 36

Late Summer Gatherings
Wall Hanging · 42

Primitive Coasters · 47

New England Hospitality Rug · 51

From the Nineteenth Century
Quilt · 55

Hole in the Barn Door Quilt · 59

Autumn Bounty Table Mat · 62

Poppies Wall Hanging · 67

Happiness Is a Bowl of Flowers
Pincushion · 70

Things I Like Best about Fall
Quilt · 73

QUILTMAKING · 77

PRIMITIVE RUG HOOKING · 88

NEEDLE FELTING · 93

RECOMMENDED READING · 94

RESOURCES · 95

ABOUT THE AUTHORS · 96

INTRODUCTION

Through this book we hope to share our love for all things primitive. For years we've both collected primitive folk art and antique quilts. This passion for all things primitive and historical has inspired us to share our own ideas and creations. This book is a reflection of Rozan's love of wool. The various colors and textures found in hand-dyed wool are her motivation in creating her rug-hooking and appliqué designs. Terry also shares an interest in wool design but her passion is quilting. All of the quilt designs in this book reflect Terry's love for and interest in antique quilts. She also finds great joy in creating homespun stitchery inspired by her life on a farm. We hope this book encourages you to create your own primitive gatherings of quilts, stitchery, wool appliqué, needle felting, and rug hooking.

—Terry and Rozan

Primitive Gatherings Quilt

Designed and piec

ere's the perfect quilt for those who love all things primitive. There are farm-fresh eggs, honey still in the skep, just-cut flowers, and even the barnyard cat. Take your time to make it and enjoy working with both homespun fabric and hand-dyed wool. Due to the primitive nature and design of this quilt, we strongly suggest that you let go of traditional quilting "rules"—this quilt is meant to be an expression of your personal tastes and creativity. We hope this quilt brings you many warm nights and plenty of comfort.

Remember, this is a primitive quilt, designed to have a scrappy look, so feel free to vary fabrics, colors, and placement. Change the colors of wool to suit your own taste. Hand-dyed wools add wonderful texture, and be sure to include some checks, tweeds, and herringbone weaves.

FINISHED SIZE: 63¾" x 70½"

Materials for Pieced Blocks, Background, and Borders

All yardages are based on 42"-wide fabric.

- 20 assorted fat quarters of homespun in light and medium plaids, stripes, and checks for half-square triangles, strips, and backgrounds
- 14 assorted fat quarters of prints or scraps for half-square triangles and blocks
- 2⅜ yards of medium gold print for outer border and binding
- 1¼ yards of light plaid homespun for background of coxcomb flower
- ½ yard of medium to light homespun for flag background
- ⅜ yard of dark plaid homespun for inner border
- ¼ yard of tan check for Church block
- ¼ yard of green print for Church block
- 1 fat quarter of black print for corner blocks
- 4 yards of fabric for backing
- 70" x 77" piece of cotton batting
- Wool thread to match appliqués

- Chenille needle, size 22
- Heavy-duty fusible web
- 505 Spray and Fix basting spray

MATERIALS FOR WOOL APPLIQUÉ
Wool yardage amounts are generously estimated and based on 54"-wide fabric. Wash new wool before using.

Assorted green wool
- ½ yard of green wool or army blanket for coxcomb stems, sawtooth borders, and pumpkin stems
- 16" x 18" piece of green for the letters
- 12" x 12" piece *each* of 4 shades of green for leaves, flower stems, and border triangles

Assorted red wool
- 10" x 24" piece of red for short flag stripes, long flag stripe, and triangles
- 9" x 12" piece *each* of 3 shades of red for stars, flowers in pitcher, and heart
- 6" x 15" piece *each* of 3 shades of red for large and small coxcomb flowers

Assorted gold wool

- 12" x 18" piece *each* of 3 shades of gold for cat stripes, cat tail tip, flag stars, large star, triangles, cart handle, floating star, and small border star

- 5" x 9" piece *each* of 4 shades of gold for bee skep
- 14" x 14" piece *each* of medium gold and dark gold for basket and flower centers

Assorted brown wool
- 8" x 12" piece of brown for church cross, cart, and border triangle
- 5" x 10" piece of brown for cart wheels
- 7" x 7" piece of brown for pitcher and pitcher handle

Assorted blue wool
- 8" x 12" piece of blue for flag star background and triangles
- 6" x 10" piece of blue for bluebird bodies
- 6" x 9" piece *each* of 2 blues for bluebird wings and floating star

Assorted orange wool
- 14" x 14" piece of orange for cat and cat nose
- 6" x 6" piece *each* of 3 shades of orange for pumpkins

Assorted black wool
- 12" x 15" piece of black for crow body, church roof, and church door
- 10" x 10" piece of black for crow wing, sheep face, sheep ear, sheep legs, cat nose, and cat eyes

Assorted wool
- 18" x 24" piece of white for church front, church steeple, eggs, and flag stripes
- 10" x 10" piece of beige or tan for sheep and eggs
- 3" x 3" piece of purple for church windows

Cutting for the Quilt

Each section of the quilt has separate cutting instructions. Be careful to keep all of the pieces for each section together. We found it easiest to cut and then sew one section at a time. When cutting the appliqués, refer to the patterns on pages 18 through 23. Most of the patterns need to be enlarged before tracing.

ROZAN'S HINT

Keep all of your cut wool appliqué pieces organized by section; it's easier to find what you need when you begin to stitch.

Section 1 Cutting: Primitive Gatherings Block and Heart and Sheep Block

From the light homespuns, cut:
- 1 rectangle, 12½" x 20"
- 1 rectangle, 8" x 9½"

From a variety of homespuns and prints, cut:
- 4 squares, 3½" x 3½"
- 26 squares, 2" x 2"

From the 16" x 18" piece of green wool, cut:
- 1 of each letter for the words *Primitive Gatherings**

From the ½ yard of green wool, cut:
- 2 short sawtooth borders*
- 2 long sawtooth borders*

From a 9" x 12" piece of red wool, cut:
- 1 heart*

From the 10" x 10" piece of beige or tan wool, cut:
- 1 sheep*

From the 10" x 10" piece of black wool, cut:
- 1 sheep face and 1 sheep ear*
- 4 sheep legs*

Use the patterns on pages 18–19.

Section 1 Assembly: Primitive Gatherings Block and Heart and Sheep Block

1. For the Primitive Gatherings block, lay out the four squares, 3½" x 3½", and sew them into a row. Press the seams in one direction.

2. Sew the unit just made to the side of the 12½" x 20" light homespun background piece. Press the seam toward the homespun.

3. To make the Heart and Sheep block, lay out the 26 squares, 2" x 2", around the 8" x 9½" light homespun rectangle. Once you're pleased with the arrangement, sew the 2" x 2" squares into two rows of seven blocks each and two rows of six blocks each. Press the seams in one direction.

4. Sew the two rows of six blocks onto the right- and left-hand sides of the 8" x 9½" rectangle. Press toward the rectangle.

5. Sew the two rows of seven blocks to the top and bottom of the 8" x 9½" rectangle. Press toward the rectangle.

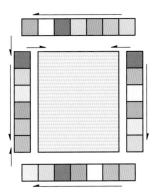

6. To complete section 1, pin the Primitive Gatherings block to the left side of the Heart and Sheep block with wrong sides together. Sew and press the seam allowance toward the Primitive Gatherings block.

7. Lay out the letters and sawtooth borders on the background of the Primitive Gatherings block. Place the sawtooth borders ¼" to ⅜" from the top and bottom raw edges to allow for the ¼" seam.

8. Referring to "Basic Steps for Wool Appliqué" on page 86, spray the appliqué pieces with 505 Spray and Fix basting spray on the wrong side and whipstitch them down. Use a thread color that matches the wool.

9. For the Heart and Sheep block, appliqué the heart and then the sheep, legs, face, and ear pieces in the same way that you appliquéd the pieces in step 8. Set the section aside.

Section 2 Cutting: Basket Block, Flowerpot Block, and Church Block

From a variety of fabrics, cut:
- 14 squares, 3⅞" x 3⅞"; cut once diagonally to yield 28 triangles

From the medium to light homespuns, cut:
- 1 rectangle, 10½" x 12½"
- 1 rectangle, 6¼" x 9"
- 1 strip, 2" x 9"
- 1 strip, 2" x 7¾"
- 1 strip, 2¼" x 10½"
- 1 rectangle, 8½" x 12½"

From the tan check, cut:
- 12 squares, 2⅞" x 2⅞"; cut once diagonally to yield 24 triangles

From the green print, cut:
- 12 squares, 2⅞" x 2⅞"; cut once diagonally to yield 24 triangles

From the 14" x 14" piece of dark gold wool, cut:
- 1 basket handle*
- 1 basket rim*
- 12 strips, ½" x 14"

From the 14" x 14" piece of medium gold wool, cut:
- 20 strips, ½" x 10"

From the 18" x 24" piece of white wool, cut:
- 4 eggs*
- 1 church front*
- 1 church steeple*

From the remainder of the 10" x 10" piece of beige or tan wool from section 1, cut:
- 2 eggs*

From a 12" x 12" piece of green wool, cut:
- 4 leaves*
- 3 flower stems*

From the 7" x 7" piece of brown wool, cut:
- 1 pitcher*
- 1 pitcher handle*

From the 8" x 12" piece of brown wool, cut:
- 1 church cross*

From the remainder of the 9" x 12" piece of red wool from section 1, cut:
- 3 flowers*

From the remainder of the 14" x 14" pieces of dark gold and medium gold wool, cut:
- 3 flower centers*

From the 12" x 15" piece of black wool, cut:
- 1 church roof*
- 1 church door*

From the 3" x 3" piece of purple wool, cut:
- 2 church windows*

Use the patterns on page 19.

Section 2 Assembly: Basket Block, Flowerpot Block, and Church Block

1. Make 14 half-square-triangle units for the Basket block and Flowerpot block using the triangles cut from the 3⅞" squares. Mix and match darker triangles with lighter triangles. Press toward the darker fabric.

Make 14.

2. For the Basket block, lay out a row of four half-square-triangle units from step 1 above and below the 10½" x 12½" rectangle of homespun. Sew the half-square-triangle units into two rows of four blocks each. Press in one direction.

3. Pin and sew the two rows of half-square-triangle units to the top and bottom of the homespun rectangle. Press toward the homespun rectangle.

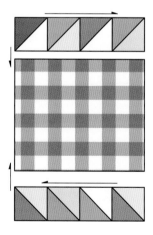

4. For the Flowerpot block, sew the 2" x 9" strip of homespun to the left side of the 6¼" x 9" rectangle of homespun. Press toward the center.

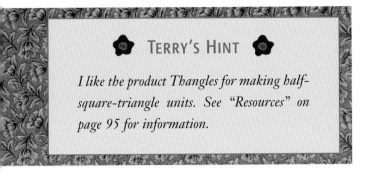

🌸 TERRY'S HINT 🌸

I like the product Thangles for making half-square-triangle units. See "Resources" on page 95 for information.

5. Sew the 2" x 7¾" homespun strip to the bottom of the unit made in step 4. Press toward the center.

6. Sew the 2¼" x 10½" strip of homespun to the right side of the unit from step 5. Press toward the center.

7. Using the remaining half-square-triangle units made in step 1, arrange three along the top of the Flowerpot block and three along the bottom. Sew into two rows and press in one direction. Sew the rows to the block; press toward the center.

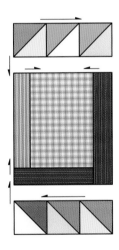

8. For the Church block, make 24 green and tan half-square-triangle units using the triangles cut from the 2⅞" squares. Press toward the darker fabric.

9. Lay out the half-square-triangle units from step 8 into four rows of six blocks each around the 8½" x 12½" homespun rectangle. Follow the illustration above right carefully to ensure that all of the colors are in the right place.

10. Sew the half-square-triangle units together into rows and press the seams in one direction. Sew the rows to the sides of the rectangle, and then add the top and bottom rows. Press toward the rectangle.

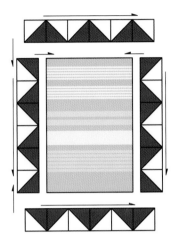

11. Assemble the three blocks into section 2, pinning and sewing the right side of the Basket block to the left side of the Flowerpot block. Press toward the Basket block. Then sew the Church block to the right side of the Flowerpot block.

12. To create the woven basket, start by laying the 12 dark gold strips next to each other horizontally as shown. Place a ½" x 10" medium gold strip in the middle of the horizontal strips and weave the vertical strips through the horizontal strips. Continue weaving the strips, pushing them together to make a tight weave.

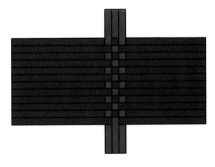

13. Trace the basket pattern (not the handle or rim) onto heavy-duty fusible web. Iron it onto the woven wool according to the product directions. Cut out the wool basket. Place the

eggs and basket handle onto the background fabric. Peel the paper backing from the fusible web and iron the basket onto the background fabric. Then place the basket rim in position. Whipstitch around the eggs, basket, basket handle, and rim. Add the remaining egg to the outside of the basket and whipstitch it down.

14. Lay out and spray-baste the appliqué pieces for the Flowerpot block and Church block, referring to the pattern and quilt photograph for placement. Remember to overlap where indicated. Adjust as needed.

15. For the Flowerpot block, whipstitch the stem and leaves first. Next, whipstitch the pitcher and handle, and then stitch the flowers and flower centers.

16. Appliqué the church front first. Then appliqué the roof, steeple, door, windows, and cross. Set the section aside.

Section 3 Cutting: Flag Block and Star Block

From the ½ yard of medium to light homespun, cut:
- 1 rectangle, 11½" x 21½"

From a light or medium homespun fat quarter, cut:
- 1 rectangle, 8½" x 9½"

From 1 medium homespun fat quarter, cut:
- 2 strips, 2" x 8½"
- 2 strips, 2" x 12½"

From a variety of prints, cut a *total* of:
- 11 squares, 3½" x 3½"

From the 10" x 24" piece of red wool, cut:
- 2 triangles*
- 2 short flag stripes*
- 1 long flag stripe*

From the remainder of the 18" x 24" piece of white wool, cut:
- 1 short flag stripe*
- 1 long flag stripe*

From the 8" x 12" piece of blue wool, cut:
- 1 star background for flag*
- 2 triangles*

From the 12" x 18" pieces of gold wool, cut:
- 3 triangles*
- 5 flag stars*
- 1 large star*

From red wool scraps, cut:
- 1 small star*

From green wool scraps, cut:
- 2 triangles*

Use the patterns on pages 20–21.

Section 3 Assembly: Flag Block and Star Block

1. For the Flag block, arrange seven squares, 3½" x 3½", cut from a variety of fabrics, in the order you like along the bottom of the 11½" x 21½" rectangle of homespun. Sew the squares together in a row. Press the seams in one direction. Sew the row of squares to the bottom of the homespun background rectangle. Press toward the background.

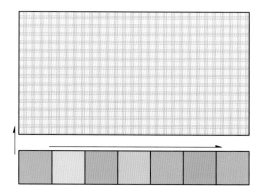

2. For the Star block, sew two 2" x 8½" strips of medium homespun to the sides of the 8½" x 9½" rectangle of homespun. Press toward the center. Sew the two 2" x 12½" strips of medium homespun to the top and bottom of the Star background. Press toward the center.

3. Sew the remaining four 3½" x 3½" squares in a row. Press the seams in one direction. Sew the row to the bottom of the Star block. Press toward the center.

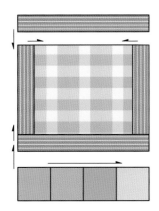

4. Sew the Flag block to the left side of the Star block. Press toward the Flag block.

5. Referring to the quilt photograph and patterns for placement, arrange the red and white stripes and blue star background onto the Flag block. Do not overlap the stripes; place them side by side. Spray-baste and whipstitch the stripes. Then whipstitch the star background.

6. Whipstitch the five gold flag stars on the blue background and stitch an X in the middle of each star.

7. For the Star block, position and whipstitch around the large gold star first. Then stitch the small red star in place. Stitch an X in the center of the small star.

8. Whipstitch the triangles randomly to the squares below the appliquéd flag and star. Set the section aside.

Section 4 Cutting: Bee Skep Block and Pumpkin Cart Block

From the light homespuns, cut:
- 1 square, 9½" x 9½"
- 1 rectangle, 12½" x 16½"

From the medium homespuns, cut:
- 2 strips, 2½" x 9½"
- 2 strips, 2" x 13½"

From the assorted homespuns and prints, cut:
- 3 squares, 4⅞" x 4⅞"; cut once diagonally to yield 6 triangles

From the four 5" x 9" pieces of gold wool, cut a *total* of:
- 1 bee skep, section 1*
- 1 bee skep, section 2*
- 1 bee skep, section 3*
- 1 bee skep, section 4*

From brown wool scraps, cut:
- 1 bee skep door*

From the 6" x 10" piece of blue wool, cut:
- 1 bluebird body*

From a 6" x 9" piece of blue wool, cut:
- 1 bluebird wing*

From the remainder of the 12" x 18" pieces of gold wool, cut:
- 1 cart handle*

From the 5" x 10" piece of dark brown wool, cut:
- 2 cart wheels*

From the remainder of the 8" x 12" piece of brown wool, cut:
- 1 cart*

From the 6" x 6" pieces of orange wool, cut:
- 3 pumpkins*

From the remainder of the ½ yard of green wool, cut:
- 3 pumpkin stems*

Use the patterns on page 21.

Section 4 Assembly:
Bee Skep Block
and Pumpkin Cart Block

1. For the Bee Skep block, sew the 2½" x 9½" medium homespun strips to the right and left sides of the 9½" x 9½" light homespun square. Press toward the center square. Sew the 2" x 13½" medium homespun strips to the top and bottom. Press toward the center.

2. Using the triangles cut from the 4⅞" squares of assorted prints and homespuns, sew three half-square-triangle units.

3. Arrange the half-square-triangle units in a row along the right side of the 12½" x 16½" rectangle of light homespun. Sew the units together and press the seams in one direction. Sew the row to the rectangle and press toward the rectangle.

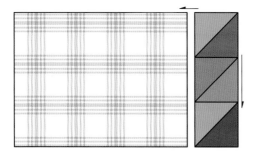

4. Sew the Bee Skep block to the left side of the Pumpkin Cart block. Press toward the Pumpkin Cart block.

5. Arrange the appliqué pieces on the Bee Skep block and Pumpkin Cart block, referring to the quilt photograph and patterns for placement. Remember to overlap where indicated.

6. Spray-baste the appliqué pieces and whipstitch the bee skep first. Then stitch the door.

7. For the Pumpkin Cart block, stitch the pumpkins first, then the green stems, the bluebird body, and the bluebird wing. Finally, whipstitch the cart, the handle, and the wheels. Set this section aside.

Section 5 Cutting:
Coxcomb Flower Block and
Half-Square-Triangle Units

From the assorted homespuns and prints, cut:
- 2 squares, 3½" x 3½"
- 1 rectangle, 2¾" x 3½"
- 32 squares, 3⅞" x 3⅞"; cut once diagonally to yield 64 triangles

From the 1¾ yards of light plaid homespun, cut:
- 1 rectangle, 14¾" x 54½"

From the remainder of the ½ yard of green wool, cut:
- 1 large coxcomb stem*
- 1 small coxcomb stem*

From the remainder of the 12" x 12" pieces of assorted green wool, cut:
- 1 lower coxcomb leaf*
- 1 middle coxcomb leaf*
- 1 upper coxcomb leaf*
- 1 small coxcomb leaf*

From one 6" x 15" piece of red wool, cut:
- 1 large coxcomb outer petal*
- 1 large coxcomb band*

Use the patterns on pages 22–23.

From a second 6" x 15" piece of red wool, cut:
- 1 large coxcomb inner petal*
- 1 small coxcomb inner petal*

From a third 6" x 15" piece of red wool, cut:
- 5 accent petals*
- 1 small coxcomb outer petal*

From the remainder of the 6" x 10" and 6" x 9" pieces of blue wool, cut:
- 1 bluebird body* reversed
- 1 bluebird wing* reversed

From the remainder of the 12" x 15" piece of black wool, cut:
- 1 crow body*

From the remainder of the 10" x 10" piece of black wool, cut:
- 1 crow wing*
- 1 cat nose*
- 2 cat eyes*

From the 14" x 14" piece of orange wool, cut:
- 1 cat*
- 1 cat upper nose*

From the remainder of the 12" x 18" pieces of gold wool, cut:
- 6 cat stripes*
- 1 cat tail tip*

From the assorted leftover scraps of blue, red, and gold wool, cut:
- 3 floating stars (1 from each color)**
- 1 border star (from gold)**

From green wool scraps, cut:
- 1 border triangle**

From brown wool scraps cut:
- 1 border triangle**

*Use the patterns on pages 21–23.

**These pieces will be appliquéd after the quilt sections are sewn together.

Section 5 Assembly: Coxcomb Flower Block and Half-Square-Triangle Units

1. Make 32 half-square-triangle units, using the 64 triangles cut from the 3⅞" squares. Press toward the darker fabric.

2. Sew a row of 14 half-square-triangle units; two squares, 3½" x 3½"; and one rectangle, 2¾" x 3½", to go across the top of the quilt blocks. Arrange them as shown, or create your own random pattern. Press the seams in one direction and set this unit aside.

2¾" x 3½" rectangle

3. Sew together a row of 18 half-square-triangle units for the left side of the Coxcomb Flower block. Arrange them randomly with the diagonals going in different directions as desired. Press the seams in one direction.

4. Sew the half-square-triangle unit row from step 3 to the long side of the 14¾" x 54½" rectangle of homespun. Press toward the homespun.

5. Arrange the appliqué pieces on the background. Refer to the quilt photograph and patterns for placement. Remember to overlap where indicated and make adjustments as needed. Some of your pieces will be hanging off the edge; these will be stitched after all the sections are sewn together.

6. Spray baste and stitch the coxcomb stem. Add the large coxcomb outer petal, accent petals, inner petal, and the band. Sew the coxcomb petals halfway, leaving the right side free. Allow enough space for the seam allowance, and pin back the extra. Then stitch the leaves. The leaf above the crow is folded and stitched down. Leave the tip of the bottom-right leaf

unsewn. Pin it back out of the way and finish sewing it later, after the sections are joined.

7. Spray-baste the remaining pieces and whip-stitch, using a thread color that matches the wool appliqué.

8. Stitch the bluebird body and wing, and add a French knot for the eye. See "Embroidery Stitches" on page 87.

9. Sew the crow's body and wing but leave his head unattached. Pin it back when you're done.

10. Stitch the cat along the bottom of the cox-comb. Leave the end of the cat's tail unstitched and pin it back. Stitch the stripes and face. Embroider the three whiskers using a backstitch.

Joining the Sections

Make sure that all of the appliqué that isn't sewn down is pinned back securely out of the way. Refer to the quilt diagram on page 17.

1. Join sections 1 and 2. Find the middle point of each section and mark it with a pin. Match up the middle points and the ends, and pin carefully. Stitch and press toward section 1, removing the pins as you come to them.

2. Join sections 3 and 4. Match the middle points and ends as you did before. Sew the sections together and press toward section 4.

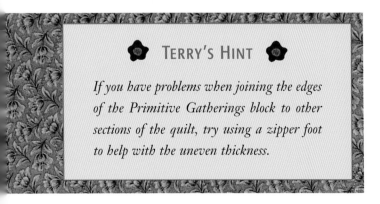

❀ TERRY'S HINT ❀

If you have problems when joining the edges of the Primitive Gatherings block to other sections of the quilt, try using a zipper foot to help with the uneven thickness.

3. In the same way, join the units from steps 1 and 2. Press toward the bottom of the quilt.

4. Join the unit from step 3 to the Coxcomb Flower block, matching the middle points and ends. Press toward the Coxcomb Flower block.

5. Sew the pieced row of half-square-triangle units and squares made in step 2 of "Section 5 Assembly" on page 15 to the top of the quilt. Press toward the center of the quilt.

6. Now you can finish the last of your appliqué. Unpin the coxcomb flower, crow, leaf, and cat's tail. Lay them out on the adjoining blocks. Spray-baste if desired and whipstitch them down.

7. Add the gold tip of the cat's tail and stitch it down.

8. Cut out a small eye for the crow from a scrap of gold wool. Stitch it down as shown.

9. Stitch the three random floating stars cut from blue, red, and gold wool scraps down where desired on the quilt top.

10. Whipstitch the two green and brown triangles and the small gold star to the squares in the pieced row along the top of the quilt.

Cutting Borders

From the dark plaid homespun, cut:
- 6 strips, 1¼" x 42"

From the medium gold print, cut:
- 7 strips, 6½" x 42"
- 16 squares, 2½" x 2½"
- 8 squares, 2⅞" x 2⅞"; cut once diagonally to yield 16 triangles

From the black print, cut:
- 4 squares, 2½" x 2½"
- 8 squares, 2⅞" x 2⅞"; cut once diagonally to yield 16 triangles

Adding Borders

1. Measure the quilt top through the center and refer to "Adding Borders" on page 80 to add the 1¼"-wide inner-border strips. Press toward the inner borders.

2. To make the corner blocks, sew 16 half-square-triangle units with the triangles cut from the black print and the medium gold print. Press toward the dark fabric.

Make 16.

3. Lay out four half-square-triangle units, one 2½" square of black print, and four 2½" squares of medium gold print as shown. Sew the rows, and then sew the block together. Press. Make four corner blocks.

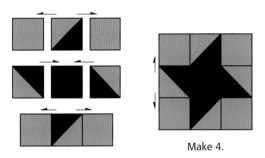

Make 4.

4. Refer to "Borders with Corner Squares" on page 80 to add the medium gold print borders and corner blocks.

Finishing

Your top is ready to quilt and bind. Refer to "Finishing the Quilt" on page 81. Then enjoy!

Enlarge patterns 200%.
Cut 2 of each sawtooth border
and 1 of each letter.

PRIMITIVE GATHERINGS

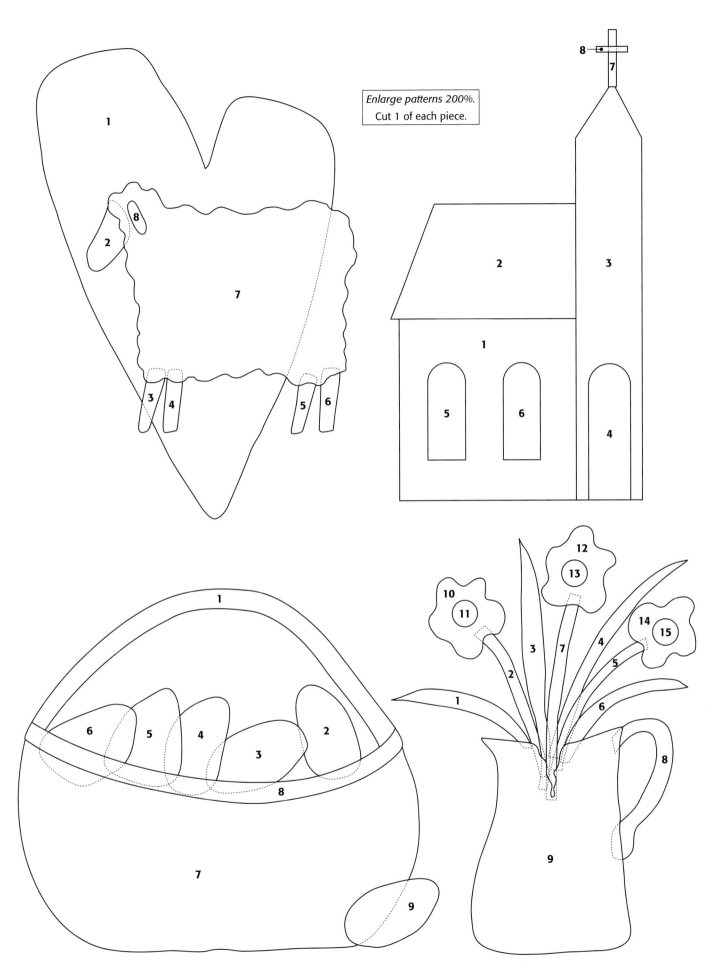

Enlarge patterns 200%.
Cut 1 of each piece.

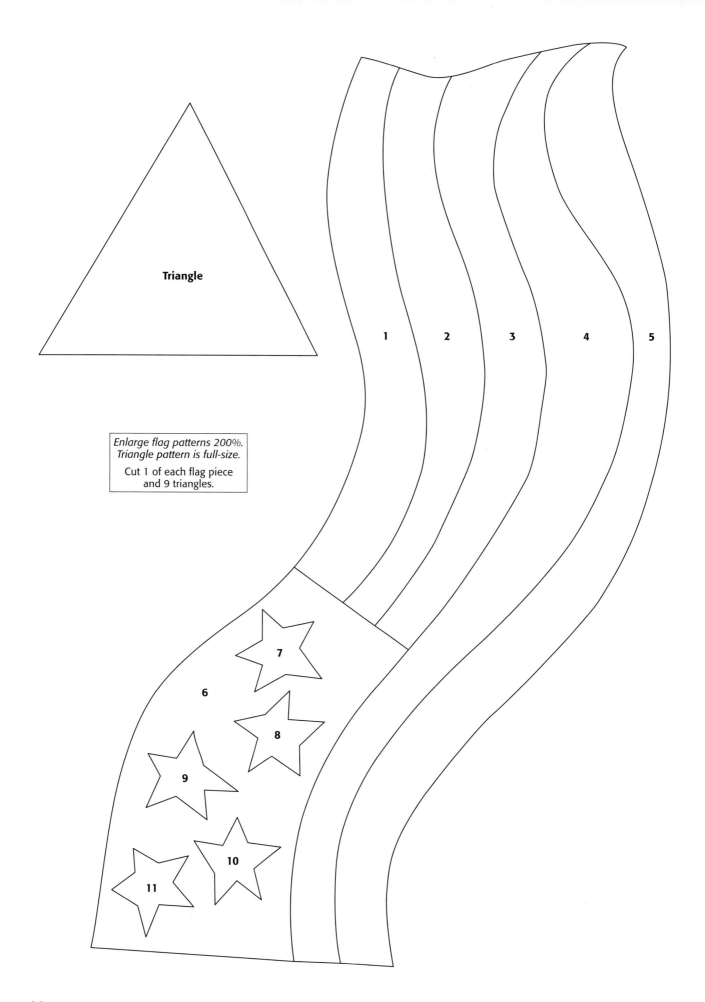

Triangle

Enlarge flag patterns 200%.
Triangle pattern is full-size.

Cut 1 of each flag piece
and 9 triangles.

1

2

3

4

5

7

6

8

9

10

11

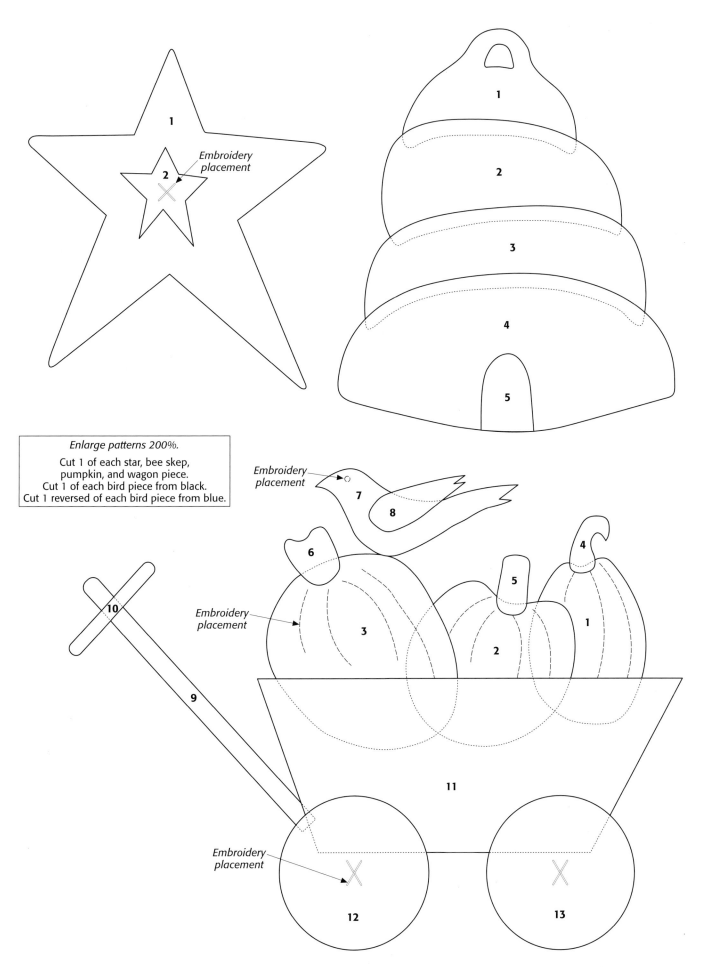

1

Embroidery placement

2

1

2

3

4

5

Enlarge patterns 200%.

Cut 1 of each star, bee skep,
pumpkin, and wagon piece.
Cut 1 of each bird piece from black.
Cut 1 reversed of each bird piece from blue.

Embroidery placement

7

8

6

4

5

Embroidery placement

3

2

1

10

9

11

Embroidery placement

12

13

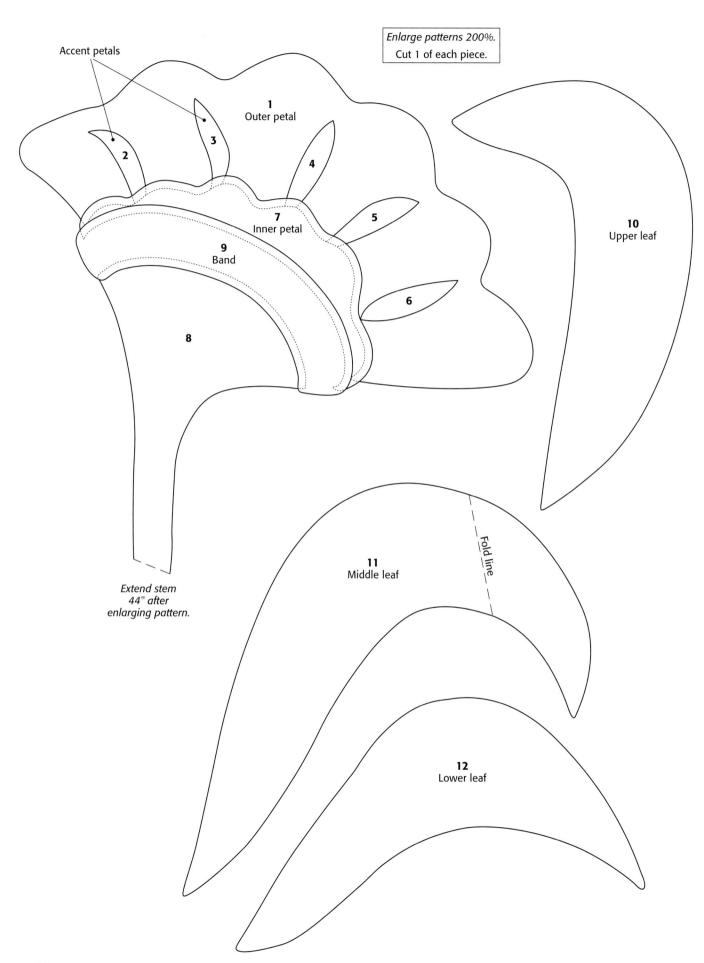

Accent petals

1
Outer petal

2

3

4

7
Inner petal

5

9
Band

6

8

Enlarge patterns 200%.
Cut 1 of each piece.

10
Upper leaf

Extend stem
44" after
enlarging pattern.

11
Middle leaf

Fold line

12
Lower leaf

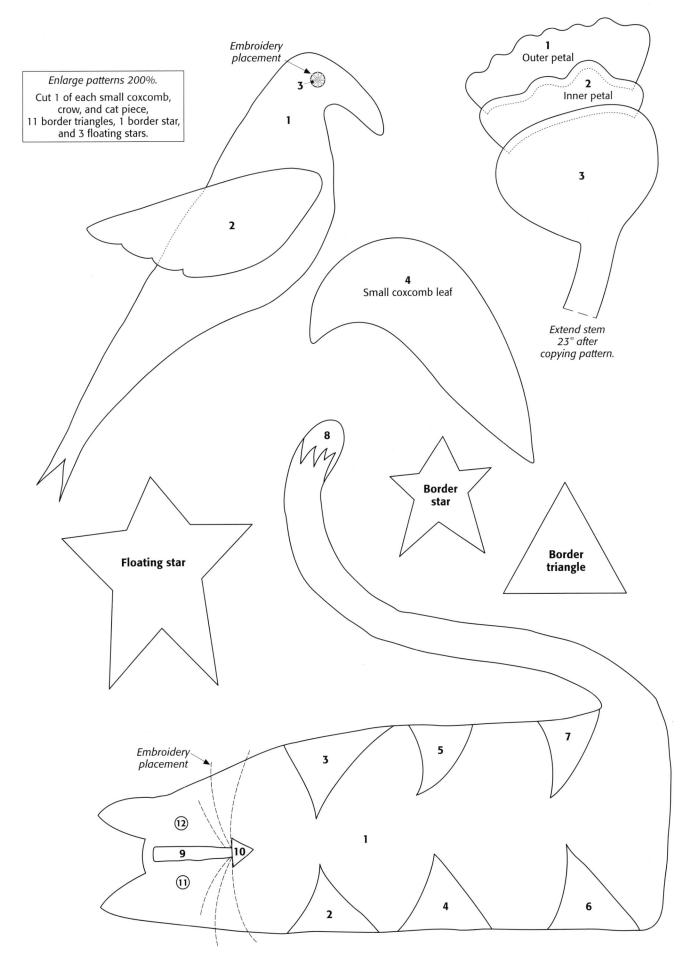

Enlarge patterns 200%.

Cut 1 of each small coxcomb, crow, and cat piece, 11 border triangles, 1 border star, and 3 floating stars.

Embroidery placement

3

1

2

1 Outer petal

2 Inner petal

3

Extend stem 23" after copying pattern.

4
Small coxcomb leaf

8

Border star

Border triangle

Floating star

Embroidery placement

3

5

7

12

9 10

11

1

2

4

6

Colors of Autumn Table Runner

W orking with wool is Rozan's passion. She loves the colors and textures that can be achieved using hand-dyed wools. Picture a handwoven basket filled with the bounty of the fall flower garden welcoming friends to your home. Set the basket arrangement on your front steps and add a whimsical crow. The silk used as the background for this table runner is also a joy to work with and it adds another texture to the wool appliqué. This project could also be done using cotton fabrics and needle-turn appliqué.

FINISHED SIZE: 18" x 44"

Materials

Wool yardage amounts are generously estimated and based on 54"-wide fabric. Wash new wool before using.

- ¾ yard of 100% matka silk for background*
- ¼ yard of gray plaid wool for baskets
- 14" x 16" piece of black wool for crows
- 14" x 14" piece of brown tweed wool for basket handles, basket handle knots, and coneflower cones
- 14" x 14" piece of light gold wool for stars and sunflower petals
- 10" x 10" piece of light green wool for coxcomb stems and leaves
- 10" x 10" piece of medium green wool for sunflower leaves
- 10" x 10" piece of dark green wool for coneflower stems, coneflower leaves, and sunflower stems
- 10" x 10" piece of purple wool for large coneflowers
- 10" x 10" piece of medium gold wool for sunflower petals and crow eyes
- 10" x 10" piece of dark gold wool for sunflower petals
- 8" x 8" piece of blue wool for crow outer wings
- 8" x 8" piece of dark red wool for large coxcombs

- 8" x 8" piece of brown-and-gold wool for sunflower centers
- 6" x 6" piece of medium red wool for large coxcomb centers and small coxcombs
- 6" x 6" piece of light purple wool for small coneflowers
- 6" x 6" piece of black plaid wool for crow inner wings
- Size 22 chenille needle *OR* size 8 embroidery needle
- 505 Spray and Fix basting spray
- Freezer paper
- Chalk marking pencil
- Wool thread and cotton thread to match the different wool

*We used Kings Road, color #269 Tobacco. You can use homespun if you prefer.

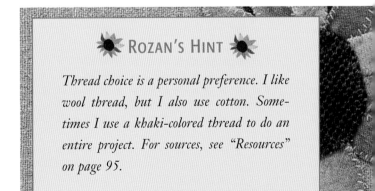

ROZAN'S HINT

Thread choice is a personal preference. I like wool thread, but I also use cotton. Sometimes I use a khaki-colored thread to do an entire project. For sources, see "Resources" on page 95.

Cutting

Enlarge and trace the pattern pieces on page 28 onto freezer paper using a black marker. Cut out the pattern pieces and iron the freezer paper onto the wool. Mark it with a chalk marking pencil and cut the pattern pieces out; do not add a seam allowance to the wool.

From the gray plaid wool, cut:
- 2 baskets

From the brown tweed wool, cut:
- 2 basket handles
- 4 basket handle knots
- 2 small coneflower cones
- 2 large coneflower cones

From the light green wool, cut:
- 2 coxcomb stems
- 6 coxcomb leaves

From the dark green wool, cut:
- 4 coneflower stems
- 6 coneflower leaves
- 2 sunflower stems

From the medium green wool, cut:
- 4 sunflower leaves

From the light gold wool, cut:
- 8 sunflower petals
- 2 stars

From the medium gold wool, cut:
- 10 sunflower petals
- 2 crow eyes

From the dark gold wool, cut:
- 6 sunflower petals

From the brown-and-gold wool, cut:
- 2 sunflower centers

From the purple wool, cut:
- 2 large coneflowers

From the light purple wool, cut:
- 2 small coneflowers

From the dark red wool, cut:
- 2 large coxcombs

From the medium red wool, cut:
- 2 large coxcomb centers
- 2 small coxcombs

From the black wool, cut:
- 2 crows

From the blue wool, cut:
- 2 crow outer wings

From the black plaid wool, cut:
- 2 crow inner wings

Preparing the Silk Background

Along both sides of the silk, find the first thread on the straight of grain that runs from selvage to selvage. Gently pull them out. Trim along each line. Wash and dry the matka silk. Cut off any long strands of thread. Using a needle, gently pull the lengthwise threads out until you have ½" of fringe on both sides. With the sewing machine and matching thread, stitch down both sides to prevent further raveling. You can also stitch a running stitch by hand with wool thread.

Appliquéing the Design

1. Using the pattern as a placement guide, position the pattern pieces at one end of the silk background. Note that a dashed line indicates that a portion of one piece is under another.

2. After placing the pieces on the background, spray the back of the pieces with the 505 Spray and Fix basting spray and replace them on the background. With this adhesive you can pick up a piece several times and move it if needed. Check the pattern for the placement of the

flowers. Some of the flowers will go under the handle and some of the flowers will go over the handle.

3. With a matching color thread, whipstitch the pieces down or use a blanket stitch, beginning with the basket. If you use any cotton fabrics, stitch them using an appliqué stitch.

4. Whipstitch the sunflower stem and leaves, and then the sunflower center and petals.

5. Whipstitch the coneflower stems, leaves, and coneflowers.

6. Whipstitch the knots from the basket handle and the coxcombs, coxcomb stems, and leaves.

7. Whipstitch the star, the crow on the basket, and the outer and inner wings to the crow.

8. Place the eye on the crow and stitch it down with black thread. Stitch across from side to

ROZAN'S HINT

My personal preference for stitching is the whipstitch. It looks like a blanket stitch but it is faster to do and doesn't use as much thread. See "Basic Steps for Wool Appliqué" on page 86 for stitch examples.

side, then from top to bottom, and then make an X stitch between those two stitches. Add a French knot in the middle of the crow's eye.

9. Repeat the stitching instructions for the other end of the silk background.

10. Make a label and attach it to the back of your table runner. Place it on your table and admire your handiwork!

Enlarge patterns 200%.
Cut 1 of each piece.

Embroidery placement

As a collector of primitive items such as pineapples, crows, bowls, and baskets made of wood, cloth, or tin, it was a given that Rozan would add a charming child's pull toy to her collection when she found it at an antique store. The charm of the wooden sheep pulled through the yard by some small child inspired her, as her treasures often do. It wasn't long before Mary's little lamb found its way into this delightful wool rug design.

FINISHED SIZE: 14" x 11"

Materials

Wool yardage amounts are generously estimated and based on 54"-wide fabric. Wash new wool before using.

- **Backing:** 22" x 19" piece of primitive linen, monk's cloth, or Scottish burlap (30" x 27" if using a hoop)
- ¼ yard of light green wool for background
- 12" x 18" piece of black wool for sheep face, sheep legs, wagon rope, star stems, outline of wagon wheels, and outer border
- 8" x 18" piece of white wool for sheep and inner border
- 8" x 18" piece of red wool for wagon, inner wheels of wagon, 2 corner squares, and inner border
- 8" x 18" piece of gold wool for star outer edges, 2 corner squares, wagon handle, and inner border
- 4" x 18" piece of off-white wool for sheep
- 4" x 18" piece of brown tweed for sheep swirls
- 4" x 18" piece of dark green wool for outer wheels of wagon and inner border
- 3" x 18" piece of light gold wool for inner stars and inner border
- 3" x 18" piece of medium green wool for S shapes in background and sheep eye

- 2 yards of dark green binding tape *OR* 1 skein of a bulky wool yarn
- Primitive rug hook
- 14" quilting hoop or rug-hooking frame
- Template plastic
- Black permanent marking pen

ROZAN'S HINT

For a small project I cut all my wool at one time, tying the colors in bunches so that they don't get tangled together. You can also put wool in plastic bags. Using plastic bags to separate your wools will help prevent the darker colors from "shedding" onto lighter colors.

Drawing the Pattern

See "Transferring the Pattern" on page 88.

1. On the piece of backing, draw a 14" x 11" rectangle with a permanent marking pen. Within the rectangle make a 13" x 10" rectangle. Draw a 1½" square in each corner and draw a line ¼" from the outer border and running from square to square for the "scrappy" inner border.

2. Make a template of the sheep, stars, and wagon using the patterns on page 32; place them on the background and trace around them with a permanent marking pen.

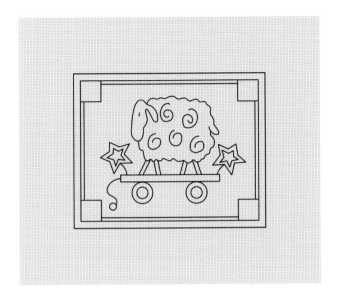

Cutting the Wool

If you're using a wool cutter, cut your wool into size 8 or 8.5 strips. If using a ruler and cutting mat, cut your strips ¼" wide. Make sure that you're cutting on the straight of grain.

Hooking Order

If you plan to use binding tape to finish this project, add it now. See "Twill Binding Tape" on page 91.

1. Hook the swirls on the sheep in brown tweed. Then outline the sheep body in white and the face and ears in black. Hook the medium green of the eye and fill in with black for the face. Use white and off-white to fill in the sheep body.

2. Hook the stars by outlining the area with the gold. Then fill in with the light gold, echoing the star shape.

3. With the black wool, hook the star stems, sheep legs, wagon rope, and outline of the wheels. Fill in the outer wheels with dark green wool.

4. Using the red wool, hook the wagon, inner wheels, and two of the corner squares.

5. Hook the two gold corner squares and the gold wagon handle.

6. Hook the outer border with black and the inner border with scraps.

7. With the medium green wool add the S shapes in the background. Fill in the background using the light green wool.

8. Finish your rug using binding tape or bulky wool yarn. See "Finishing the Rug" on page 91.

9. Make a label and attach it to the back.

Enlarge pattern 150% to 11" x 14".
One square equals ½".

Rules for Country Living Wall Hanging

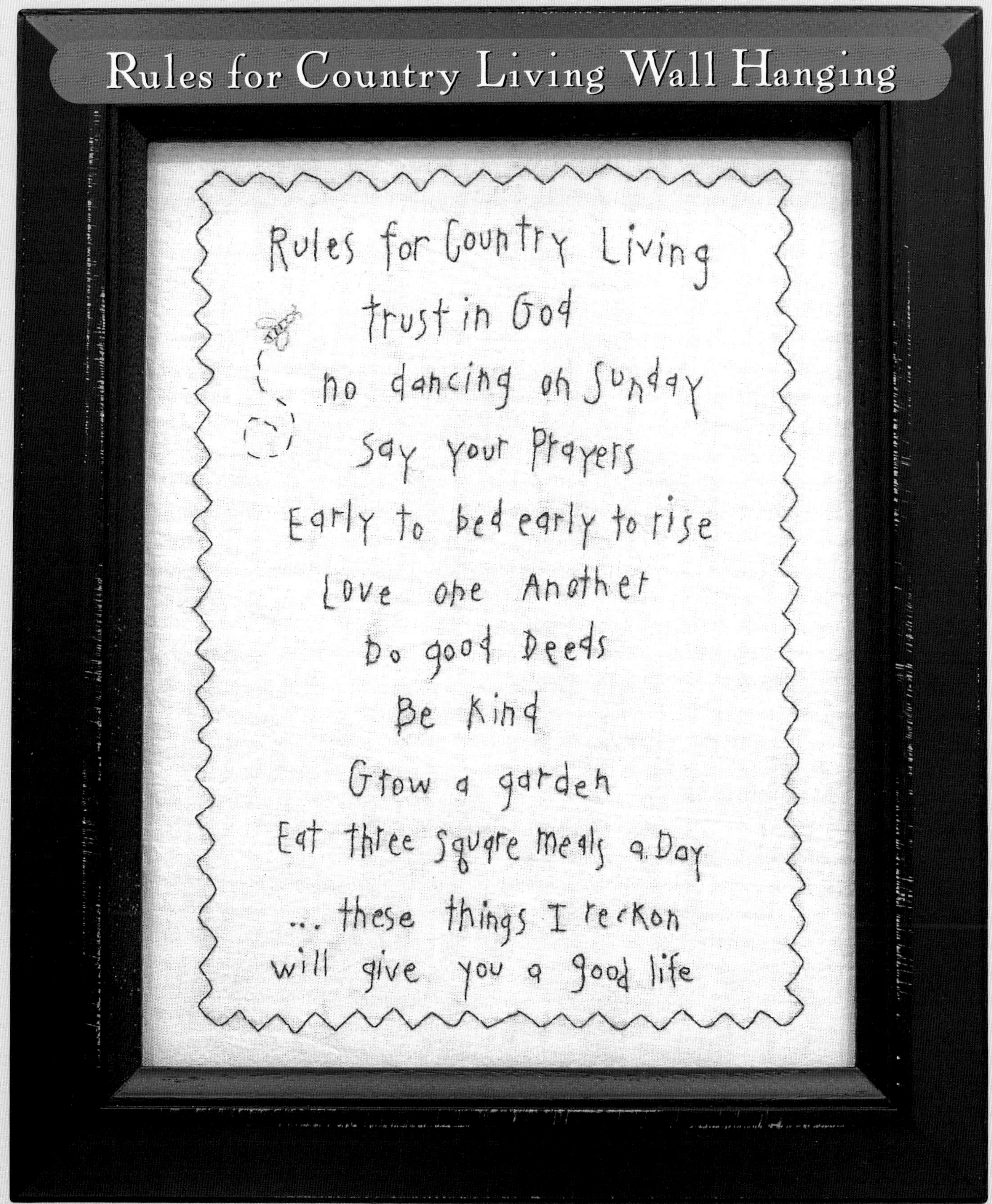
Rules for Country Living
trust in God
no dancing on Sunday
say your Prayers
Early to bed early to rise
Love one Another
Do good Deeds
Be Kind
Grow a garden
Eat three square meals a Day
... these things I reckon
will give you a good life

The primitive stitching and aged look of this rule sheet are reflective of the country life. One can sense the good nature of people and the allure of the countryside within Terry's charming stitchery. So be sure to follow the rules and "these things I reckon will give you a good life."

Materials

- 12" x 14" piece of tea-dyed muslin or osnaburg
- 1 skein of *Weeks Dye Works* Charcoal or DMC 310 (Black) floss for lettering and border
- 1 skein of *Weeks Dye Works* Whisky or DMC 3820 (Gold) floss for bee
- Embroidery needle
- Embroidery hoop
- Brown Pigma pen, size .005, or water-soluble marker
- Light box (optional)
- Frame with 8" x 10" opening

Stitching Directions

1. Using a light box and Pigma pen or marker, transfer the pattern on page 35 onto the 12" x 14" piece of muslin or osnaburg. Keep the lines as fine as possible.

2. Using one strand of Charcoal or Black floss, stitch the lettering with a backstitch; stitch the bee with Charcoal or Black and Whisky or Gold. Use French knots to dot each letter *i* and make the punctuation. Refer to "Embroidery Stitches" on page 87 for stitch instructions.

3. If you have used a water-soluble marker, soak the finished piece in water to remove the markings. Lay it flat to dry and press gently with an iron from the wrong side.

Finishing

Mount your stitchery on acid-free paperboard and insert it into the frame.

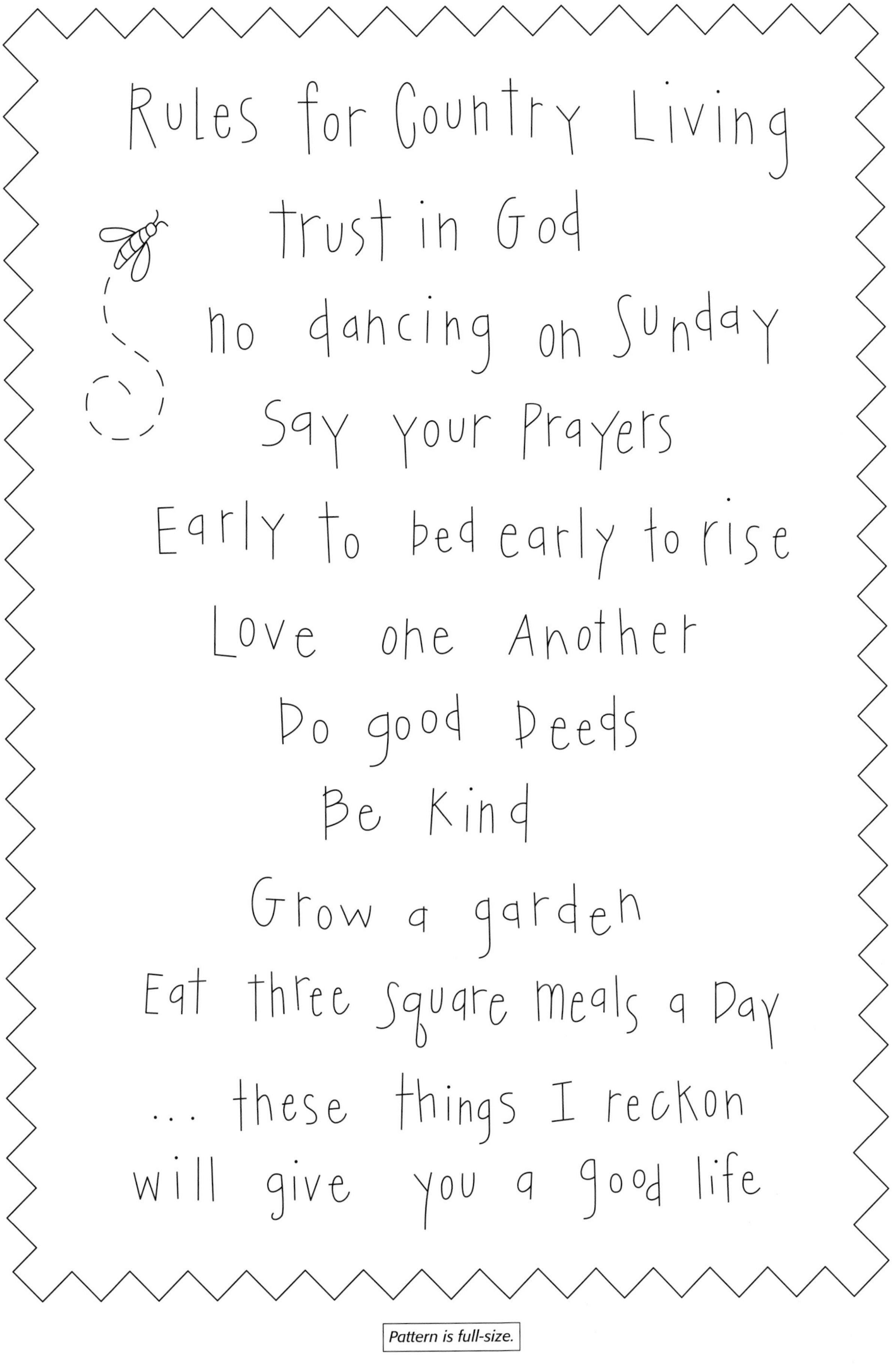

Rules for Country Living

trust in God

no dancing on Sunday

Say your Prayers

Early to bed early to rise

Love one Another

Do good Deeds

Be Kind

Grow a garden

Eat three square meals a Day

... these things I reckon
will give you a good life

Pattern is full-size.

Country Homecoming Quilt

Pieced by Terry Burkhart, appliquéd by MaryLynn Konyu and Rozan Meacham, and quilted by Martha Dirks

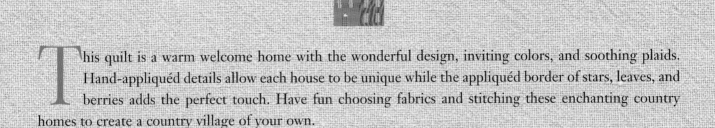

This quilt is a warm welcome home with the wonderful design, inviting colors, and soothing plaids. Hand-appliquéd details allow each house to be unique while the appliquéd border of stars, leaves, and berries adds the perfect touch. Have fun choosing fabrics and stitching these enchanting country homes to create a country village of your own.

FINISHED QUILT: 50" x 63" • FINISHED BLOCK: 12" x 12"

Materials

All yardages are based on 42"-wide fabric.

- 12 assorted fat eighths in light prints for backgrounds
- 12 assorted fat eighths for chimneys and roofs
- 12 assorted fat eighths for house fronts
- 12 assorted fat eighths for house sides
- 1⅝ yards of dark fabric for borders and sashing
- ⅝ yard of dusty green fabric for vines and leaves
- Scraps for windows, doors, and shutters
- Gold scraps for stars
- Red scraps for berries
- ⅝ yard of fabric for binding
- 3¼ yards of fabric for backing
- 57" x 71" piece of batting

Cutting

From *each* house background fabric, cut:
- 2 A rectangles, 2½" x 3½"
- 1 B rectangle, 2½" x 4"
- 2 C squares, 3½" x 3½"

From *each* chimney and roof fabric, cut:
- 2 D rectangles, 1¾" x 2½"
- 1 E rectangle, 3½" x 9½"

From *each* house front fabric, cut:
- 2 F squares, 3½" x 3½"
- 1 G rectangle, 6½" x 7½"

From *each* house side fabric, cut:
- 1 H rectangle, 6½" x 7½"

From the dark fabric, cut:
- 8 strips, 1¾" x 12½"
- 3 strips, 1¾" x 39"
- 6 strips, 6" x 42"

Making the Blocks

1. Using a ¼" seam allowance for all piecing, sew together fabric pieces A, D, B, D, and A in consecutive order along the 2½" edges as shown. Press toward the dark D pieces.

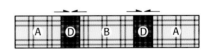

2. Place one C square and one F square right sides together. On the wrong side of the lighter square, draw a line diagonally from one corner to the other; stitch on the drawn line. Trim off one side, leaving a ¼" seam allowance. Press toward C.

3. Place one C square on the right end of an E rectangle and one F square on the left end, right sides together. Draw a line diagonally on the wrong side of the C square from top left to bottom right and stitch on the drawn line. Repeat with square F as shown. Trim off the outer corners, leaving a ¼" seam allowance. Press toward C and F. This creates the roof unit.

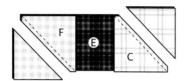

4. Place the G rectangle and the H rectangle right sides together and sew along the 7½" side. Press toward the H rectangle. This unit creates the front of the house. The G rectangle should be on the left and the H rectangle on the right.

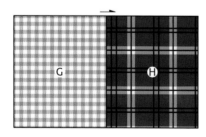

5. Sew the C and F half-square-triangle unit from step 2 to the left of the roof unit; press toward the C and F unit.

6. Sew the units together as shown to make a House block. Press.

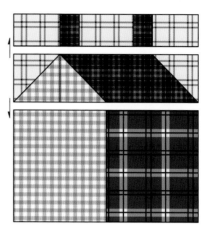

7. Repeat steps 1 through 6 to make 12 House blocks.

8. Appliqué the finishing touches on the houses. Using the patterns on page 40, make templates and cut out windows, doors, and shutters from scraps left over from the blocks. Lay out the appliqués in a pleasing arrangement. Once you're happy with the placement, appliqué the windows, doors, and shutters to the blocks. Refer to "Hand Appliqué: Needle-Turn Method" on page 82.

Assembling the Quilt Top

1. Lay out four rows of three House blocks per row, with 1¾" x 12½" sashing strips between the blocks as shown. Sew the blocks and sashing together. Press toward the sashing.

2. Sew the rows together with the long 1¾" x 39" sashing strips. Press toward the sashing.

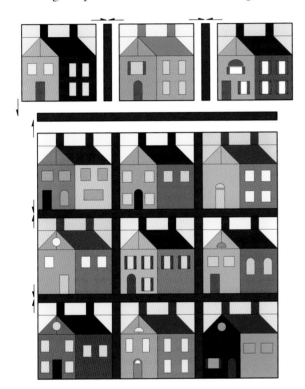

3. For the border, sew the six 6"-wide strips together end to end with diagonal seams to make one long piece. Carefully measure through the center of the quilt from top to bottom. Cut two strips from the long border strip to this length. Sew these strips to the left and right sides of the quilt top. Press toward the borders. Refer to "Adding Borders" on page 80 for additional details if needed.

4. Measure through the center of the quilt from side to side, including the borders just added. Cut two strips from the remainder of the border strip to this length. Sew the border strips to the top and bottom of the quilt top. Press toward the borders.

Appliquéing the Border

1. From the dusty green fabric, cut 14 strips of ¾"-wide bias strips, each approximately 16" long.

2. Using the patterns on page 41, make templates for the berries, leaves, and stars. Cut berries from red scraps, cut stars from gold scraps, and cut the leaves from the dusty green scraps.

3. Pin the vines in place on the border, using the photograph on page 36 as a guide. Use needle-turn appliqué, turning under ⅛" as you stitch, or use your preferred method to stitch

the vines in place. The vines should be ½"
wide when finished.

4. Appliqué the stars over the ends of the vines.
   Arrange the berries and leaves in a pleasing
   fashion and appliqué them to the border.

Finishing

Your top is ready to quilt and bind! Refer to
"Finishing the Quilt" on page 81. Hang it on the
wall or display it where all can enjoy!

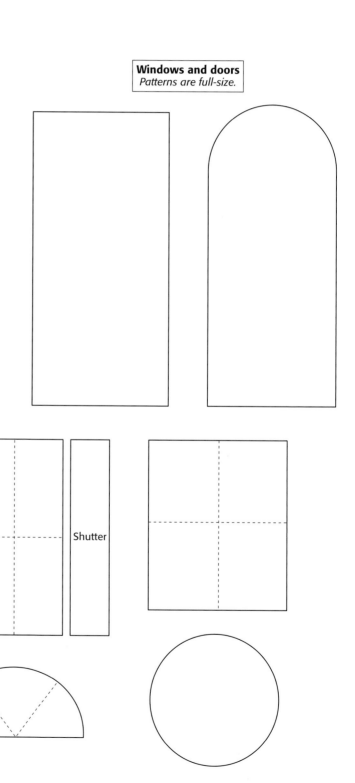

Windows and doors
Patterns are full-size.

Shutter   Shutter

*Optional
stitching detail*

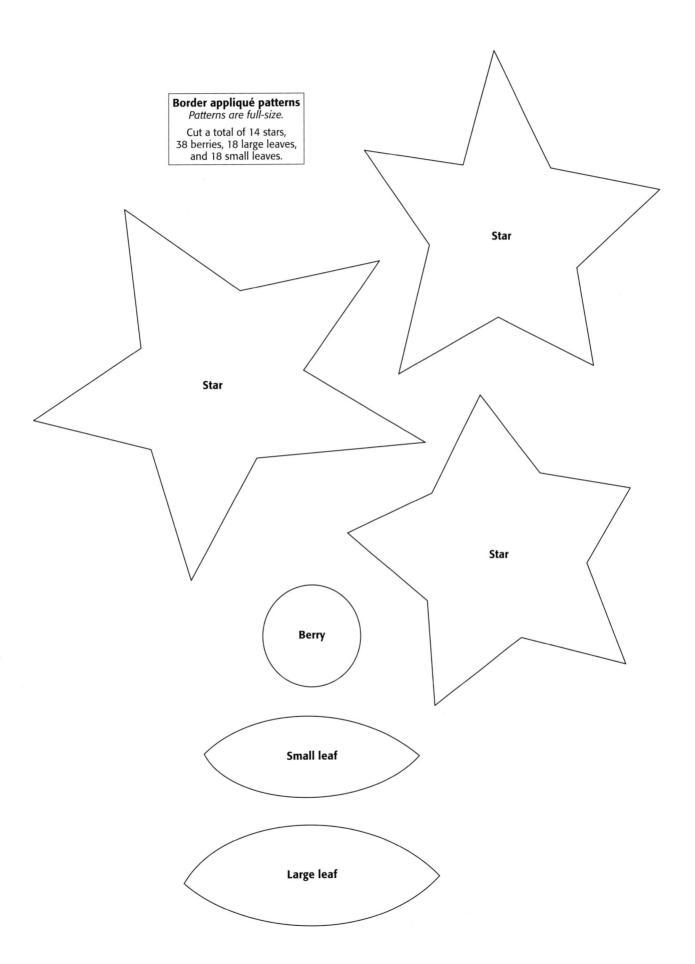

Border appliqué patterns
Patterns are full-size.

Cut a total of 14 stars,
38 berries, 18 large leaves,
and 18 small leaves.

Star

Star

Star

Berry

Small leaf

Large leaf

Late Summer Gatherings Wall Hanging

It's late summer and fall is just around the corner. The sunflowers are shining their golden faces and the purple coneflowers are displaying their last glorious blooms. Rozan arranged a gathering of these last beautiful blossoms in an old sap bucket that her daughters brought from New England. Then she placed them on the dining-room table and added one of her beloved stuffed crows. This provided the inspiration for the captivating wall hanging you see here.

FINISHED SIZE: 22" x 25"

Materials

All yardages are based on 42"-wide fabric.

- ¾ yard of black-and-tan check for background and binding
- 1 fat quarter *each* of medium green print and dark green solid for leaves and stems
- ⅜ yard of brown print for outer border
- ⅜ yard of black fabric for inner border and crow body
- 1 fat quarter of red print for sap bucket and handle
- 1 fat eighth *each* of light gold print and dark gold print for sunflower petals and crow beak
- 5" x 5" piece *each* of light purple print and medium purple print for coneflowers
- 5" x 5" piece of gold print for star
- 5" x 5" piece of black fabric with dots for sunflower center
- Scraps of brown print for coneflower cones
- Scraps of black print for crow wing
- ¾ yard of fabric for backing
- 26" x 29" piece of lightweight cotton batting
- Freezer paper
- Appliqué needle or straw needle, size 10
- Thread to match appliqué fabrics
- Roxanne's Glue-Baste-It
- Chalk pencil

Cutting

Enlarge the patterns on page 46 and make freezer-paper templates for the appliqué shapes. Iron the shapes onto the right side of the fabric and trace around them using a marking pencil. Cut them out, adding ¼" seam allowances. Note that the background is cut oversize to allow for some shrinkage from the appliqué and will be cut to size later.

From the black-and-tan check, cut:
- 1 piece, 16" x 19"

From the red print, cut:
- 1 sap bucket
- 1 handle

From the dark green solid, cut:
- 2 coneflower stems
- 1 sunflower leaf

From the light purple print, cut:
- 1 large coneflower

From the medium purple print, cut:
- 1 small coneflower

From the brown print scraps, cut:
- 1 large coneflower cone
- 1 small coneflower cone

From the medium green print, cut:
- 2 coneflower leaves

From the light gold print, cut:
- Sunflower petals #13, #15, #16, #18, #19, #21, and #22
- 1 crow beak

From the dark gold print, cut:
- Sunflower petals #12, #14, #17, and #20

From the black fabric with dots, cut:
- 1 sunflower center

From the black fabric, cut;
- 2 strips, 1½" x 18"
- 2 strips, 1½" x 17"
- 1 crow body

From the black print, cut:
- 1 crow wing

From the gold print, cut:
- 1 star

From the brown print for outer border, cut:
- 2 strips, 3" x 20"
- 2 strips, 3" x 22"

Appliquéing the Design

Use your favorite appliqué method or refer to "Hand Appliqué: Needle-Turn Method" on page 82 and follow the instructions.

1. Using the pattern as a guide, place the pieces on the black-and-tan background fabric, beginning with the sap bucket and handle. A dotted line on the pattern means that part of the pattern is under another object.

2. Add the two stems for the coneflowers; the large one will be under the handle and the short one over the handle.

3. Add the two coneflowers, the cones, and the coneflower leaves.

4. Add the sunflower leaf, sunflower petals, and sunflower center.

5. Add the crow body, crow beak, crow wing, and star.

6. Using Roxanne's Glue-Baste-It, add little dots of glue behind each piece. Then appliqué your pieces down with matching thread for each piece. You can place one piece at a time and then stitch—it depends on how you like to appliqué.

7. To make the crow's eye, use yellow thread and sew two straight stitches to make a plus sign (+). Then add two more lines to make an X over the plus sign.

8. After the appliqué is complete, trim the background piece to 15" x 18".

Assembling the Quilt Top and Finishing

1. Sew the 1½" x 18" black inner-border strips to the sides of the center block; sew the 1½" x 17" strips to the top and bottom. Press toward the black strips.

2. Sew the 3" x 20" brown print strips to the sides of the quilt. Sew the 3" x 22" brown print strips to the top and bottom of the quilt.

3. See "Finishing the Quilt" on page 81 to layer the quilt top, batting, and backing together.

4. Rozan echo quilted her project by machine. To do this, begin just outside the design and sew around it. Move ½" from your first row of stitching and go around again. Repeat this process, extending the stitching into the borders until you're finished.

5. Use a chalk marking pencil to randomly mark scallops around the outside of the brown print border. The scallops are random and not meant to be perfect or symmetrical. Use a rotary cutter to trim along the scalloped edges.

6. Use a bias binding to bind the curved edges. With a rotary cutter and mat, cut 2¼"-wide strips of black-and-tan check on the bias at 45°. Refer to "Binding" on page 81. Sew the ends together to make a continuous long strip. Fold the strip in half lengthwise, wrong sides together, and press.

7. Attach the binding to your quilt.

8. Make a label and sew it to the back of your quilt.

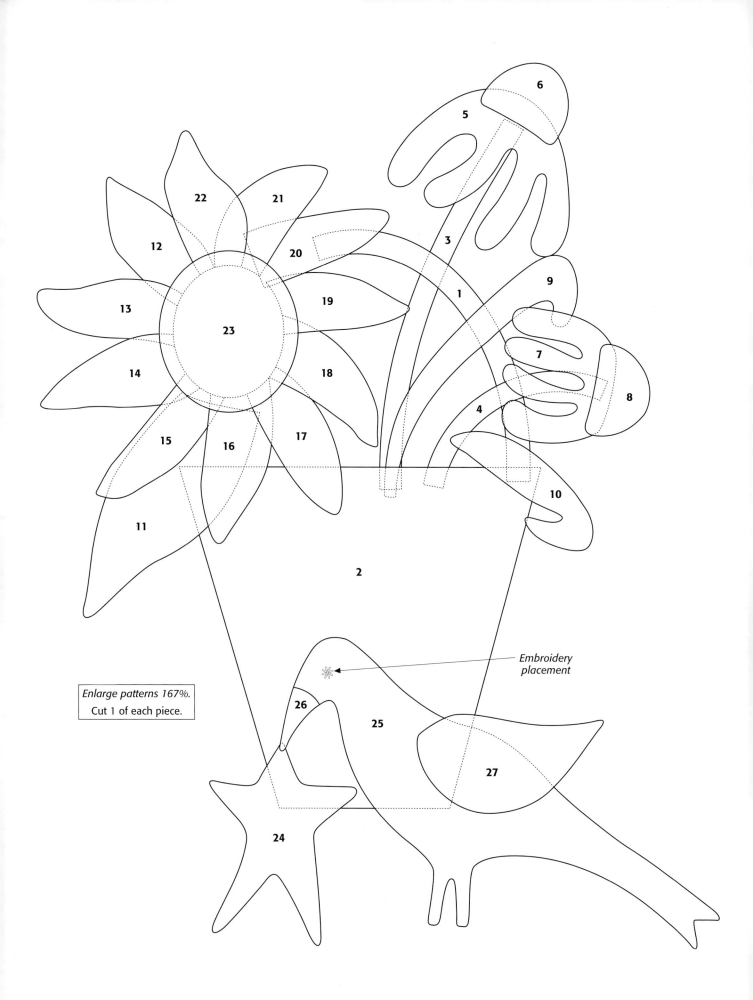

6

5

3

22

21

12

20

9

13

19

23

7

14

18

8

4

15 16 17

10

11

2

Enlarge patterns 167%.
Cut 1 of each piece.

Embroidery
placement

26

25

27

24

R ozan and her friends get together for fellowship and fragrant cups of tea at least once a week. Since Rozan loves working and designing with wool, she naturally became enamored with the texture and the primitive look of needle-felted wool. It was a great joy for her to design these primitive wool coasters. She and her friendship group place their teacups on them when they gather to study the Bible.

FINISHED SIZE: 4" diameter

Materials for 6 Coasters

Materials are based on ½-ounce balls of wool roving.

- 12" x 18" piece of brown-and-black check wool for backing
- 10" x 15" piece of tan wool for background
- 1 ball of orange wool roving for pumpkin and oak leaf
- 1 ball of green wool roving for leaves and stems
- 1 ball of red wool roving for star and flower
- 1 ball of black wool roving for crow
- 1 ball of gold wool roving for crow and pineapple
- 1 ball of brown wool roving for pineapple and acorn
- Template plastic
- Fine-tip, black permanent marking pen
- Felting needles and foam
- Black wool thread or floss
- Chalk marking pencil
- Fabric adhesive spray
- Tapestry needle

Cutting for 6 Coasters

Make circle templates using the patterns on page 49.

From the tan wool, cut:
- 6 background circles

From the brown-and-black check wool, cut:
- 6 backing circles

Making the Coasters

Refer to "Needle Felting" on page 93 before beginning this project.

1. Trace the patterns on pages 49–50 onto template plastic and cut them out.

2. Trace the background circles and design patterns onto the tan background with a marking pen or chalk pencil. You can cut the circles out now or wait until the felting is complete.

3. For the star, use a small amount of red roving to fill in the area of the star. With the felting needle, make quick stabs into the roving. Use the tapestry needle to mold the roving into a star while the other hand is making quick stabs into the roving. To get a smooth finish, make many shallow stabs. Add more roving to build the star. Don't stab too far into the foam or you may break your needle.

4. Repeat the process to felt the flower, crow, pumpkin, acorn, oak leaf, stems, leaves, and the pineapple. To create the veins on the pineapple, take a long thin piece of the brown roving and twist it in your hand to make a very thin piece. Attach the top of the roving to the pineapple and twist it as you make your line, stabbing it in place with the needle. Use the same procedure to create other narrow accent lines. On the pumpkin, use lighter or darker roving to make the veins. For the crow, work in a little gold roving to create definition between the bird body and the wing.

5. Press your designs with a steam iron set on wool and lots of steam. Place a linen or cotton cloth on the right side and press.

6. Spray a little fabric adhesive on the wrong side of the coaster background and center it over the backing. The adhesive will anchor it down while you sew around the edge. Trim your backing a little if needed. Fold the backing around to the front of the coaster. Use black thread and sew a straight running stitch around the coaster. The coaster may buckle a little after stitching; use the steam iron and pressing cloth to press it flat.

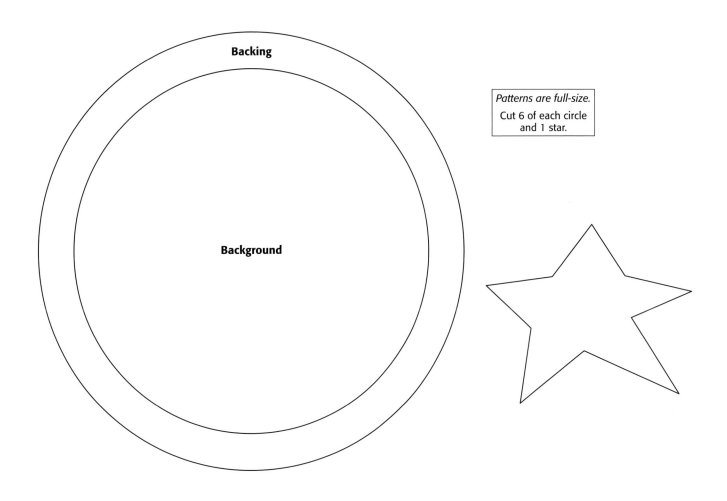

Backing

Background

Patterns are full-size.
Cut 6 of each circle
and 1 star.

Patterns are full-size.
Cut 1 of each appliqué piece.

Roving
placement

Roving
placement

When pineapples first arrived in the colonies in the early 1700s, they were hard to obtain and expensive, so when a hostess served a pineapple, you were an honored guest indeed. The pineapple soon became the symbol of warmth, charm, and hospitality throughout the colonies. Rozan collects antique and primitive wood, tin, and wool pineapples, and a pineapple wool rug is the perfect way to welcome friends and family to her home. This adaptable design can be used as a wall hanging, a table accent, or a chair pad. Whenever possible, use hand-dyed wools; they add texture and depth to your design.

FINISHED SIZE: 10" diameter

Materials

Wool yardage amounts are generously estimated and based on 54"-wide fabric. Wash new wool before using.

- **Backing:** 18" x 18" piece of primitive linen, monk's cloth, or Scottish burlap (26" x 26" if using a hoop)
- ¼ yard of black-and-brown check wool for background
- ⅛ yard of light gold wool for pineapple
- 4" x 18" piece of dark gold wool for veins of pineapple
- 4" x 18" piece of red wool for star background
- 4" x 18" piece of purple wool for star and background swirls
- 3" x 18" piece of medium green wool for pineapple leaves and center of pineapple diamonds
- 3" x 18" piece of light green wool for pineapple leaves
- 3" x 18" piece of dark green wool for pineapple leaves
- 25 yards of variegated (purple, black, and brown) 100% bulky wool yarn OR 2 yards of black binding tape
- Primitive rug hook
- 14" quilting hoop or rug-hooking frame
- Template plastic
- Black permanent marking pen

Drawing the Pattern

See "Preparing the Backing" on page 88.

1. On the piece of backing, draw a 10⅛"-diameter circle with a permanent marker.

2. Enlarge the pattern on page 54, and make templates for the pineapple, leaves, star background, and star. Using the pattern as a guide, position the templates on the backing inside the circle and trace around them with a black marking pen.

Cutting the Wool

If you're using a cutter, cut your wool into size 8 or 8.5 strips. If using a ruler and cutting mat, cut your strips ¼" wide. Make sure that you're cutting on the straight of the grain.

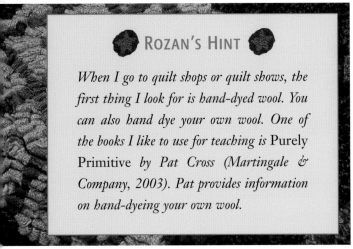

ROZAN'S HINT

When I go to quilt shops or quilt shows, the first thing I look for is hand-dyed wool. You can also hand dye your own wool. One of the books I like to use for teaching is Purely Primitive *by Pat Cross (Martingale & Company, 2003). Pat provides information on hand-dyeing your own wool.*

Hooking Order

If you plan to use binding tape to finish this project, add it now. See "Twill Binding Tape" on page 91.

1. Hook the veins on the pineapple, and then hook one medium green loop in the center of each diamond. Fill in the diamond shapes with the light gold wool.

2. Hook the star, outlining the area first. Then fill it in, echoing the star shape. Next, hook the background of the star.

3. To give the green leaves highlights, hook the leaves using the light green, medium green, and dark green wools.

4. Hook one outside row with the black-and-brown check to create the outer border. Add the squiggly lines in the background with purple wool before you fill in the background with the black-and-brown check.

5. Finish the rug using the binding tape or whipstitch with the variegated purple, black, and brown wool yarn. See "Finishing the Rug" on page 91.

6. Make a label and attach it to the back.

Enlarge pattern 150% to 10⅛" x 10⅛".
One square equals ½".

Pieced and quilted by Terry Burkhart

Terry's inspiration for this quilt is rooted deep in the Civil War. This unpretentious Nine Patch pattern resembles quilts that were given to soldiers as they recovered at the wartime hospitals. These quilts comforted men while they were restored to health and gave them a little touch of home when they were so far away. Don't prewash your fabrics if you want to wash the finished quilt for an antique look.

FINISHED QUILT: 70" x 70" • FINISHED BLOCK: 4½" x 4½"

Materials

All yardages are based on 42"-wide fabric.

- 3⅛ yards of muslin for blocks
- 33 strips, 6½" x 21", of assorted print fabrics for blocks
- ¾ yard of brown print for outer border
- ⅜ yard of blue print for inner border
- ¾ yard of fabric for binding
- 4¼ yards of fabric for backing
- 76" x 76" piece of batting

Cutting

From *each* print strip, cut:
- 3 squares, 6" x 6", to yield a total of 99 squares (You will have 1 left over.)

From the muslin, cut:
- 98 squares, 6" x 6"

From the blue print, cut:
- 7 strips, 1¼" x 42"

From the brown print, cut:
- 7 strips, 3" x 42"

Making the Blocks

1. Pair each 6" square of print fabric with a 6" square of muslin, right sides together. You'll have 98 pairs. Sew ¼" from the right and left sides of each pair.

Make 98.

2. Rotary cut this unit into three rectangles, each measuring 2" x 6". Press the seams toward the prints in the pieced units.

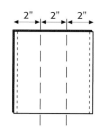

3. Sew a print center rectangle from step 2 to a pieced unit and a muslin center rectangle to a pieced unit as shown. Press toward the prints. Make 98 of each unit.

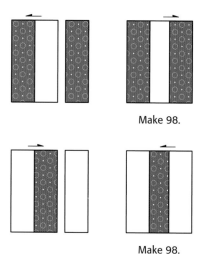

Make 98.

Make 98.

4. Pair the square units from step 3 right sides together and sew along the top and bottom using a ¼" seam. You are working with the same fabrics, one print and one muslin, to create two blocks. Terry made a few renegade blocks, mixing the units for interest.

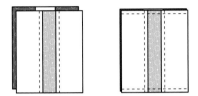

5. Cut these squares into three 2" x 6" rectangles as you did in step 2. Sew the center rectangle units to the two-rectangle units as shown. From each pair of 6" squares, you now have two 5" x 5" Nine Patch blocks. Press the seams as shown. You should have 98 of each block.

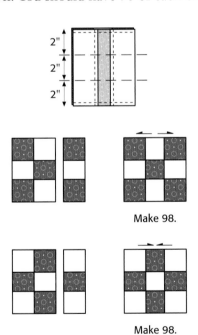

Make 98.

Make 98.

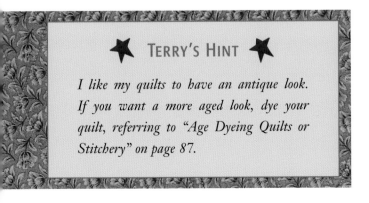

★ TERRY'S HINT ★

I like my quilts to have an antique look. If you want a more aged look, dye your quilt, referring to "Age Dyeing Quilts or Stitchery" on page 87.

Assembling the Quilt Top

1. Refer to the quilt diagram and lay out your blocks. Begin the first row with a block with muslin corners in the left position and end with a block with dark corners on the right. There will be 14 blocks per row.

2. Alternating the blocks, lay them out in rows until you have 14 rows and are pleased with the color arrangement.

3. Sew the blocks together in rows, pressing the seams in opposite directions from row to row.

4. Sew the rows together and press the seams in one direction.

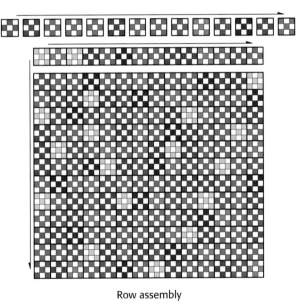

Row assembly

5. Sew the seven 1¼"-wide blue print inner-border strips together end to end with a diagonal seam to make one long strip. Carefully measure through the center of the quilt from the top to bottom. Cut two strips from the long border strip to this length. Sew these strips to the left and right sides of the quilt top. Press toward the borders.

6. Measure through the center of the quilt from side to side, including the borders that you just added. Cut two strips to this length from the remainder of the long border strip and sew

them to the top and bottom of the quilt. Press toward the borders.

7. Sew the seven 3"-wide brown print outer-border strips together end to end on a diagonal to make one long strip. Measure the quilt through the center. Cut and sew the borders to the quilt as you did for the inner border.

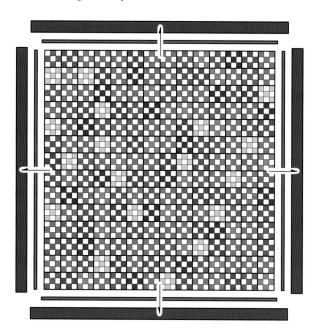

Finishing

1. Terry machine quilted the Nine Patch blocks diagonally through the muslin squares using a walking foot and natural-colored thread. She used the scallop design at right to mark the border and quilted it with a walking foot.

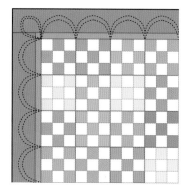

2. Referring to "Binding" on page 81, sew the binding to your quilt.

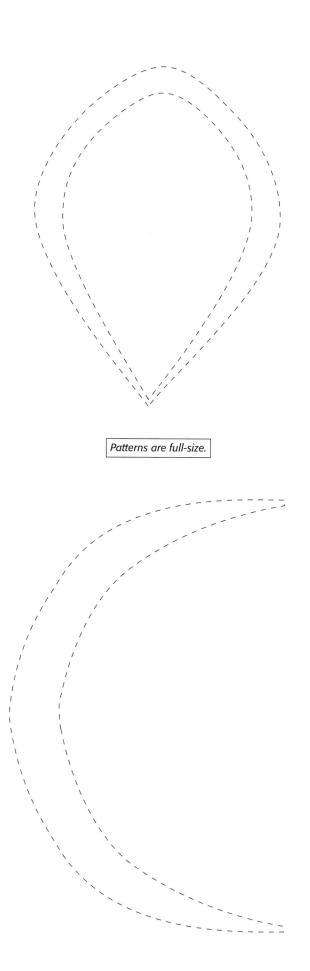

Patterns are full-size.

Hole in the Barn Door Quilt

Pieced and quilted by Terry Burkhart

C ome and take a peek through Terry's "Hole in the Barn Door." You'll see the warmth and comfort of the country displayed in this charming traditional pattern. This quilt will transport you back to the farm in no time with its nostalgic colors and homespun feel. What more could you ask for?

FINISHED QUILT: 52½" x 63" • FINISHED BLOCK: 8½" x 8½"

Materials

All yardages are based on 42"-wide fabric.

- 1 fat eighth (9" x 22") *each* of 20 tan prints for block backgrounds
- 1 fat eighth *each* of 20 red prints for blocks
- 1⅛ yards of medium tan print for sashing
- ⅞ yard of brown print for border
- ¼ yard of tan plaid for sashing cornerstones
- ⅝ yard of fabric for binding (¾ yard if cut on bias)
- 3⅜ yards of fabric for backing
- 59" x 69" piece of cotton batting

Cutting

From *each* tan fat eighth, cut:
- 2 squares, 4⅜" x 4⅜"
- 4 rectangles, 2" x 2¼"
- 1 square, 2" x 2"

From *each* red fat eighth, cut:
- 2 squares, 4⅜" x 4⅜"
- 4 rectangles, 2" x 2¼"

From the medium tan print, cut*:
- 25 rectangles, 2½" x 9", on the lengthwise grain
- 24 rectangles, 2½" x 9", on the crosswise grain

From the tan plaid, cut:
- 30 squares, 2½" x 2½"

From the brown print, cut:
- 6 strips, 4½" x 42"

*If your sashing print is not directional, you can cut all 49 rectangles on the crosswise grain.

Making the Blocks

1. For one block, make four half-square-triangle units. Draw a diagonal line from corner to corner on the wrong side of two tan 4⅜" tan squares. Pair each square with a red print 4⅜" square and layer them with right sides together. Stitch ¼" from either side of the diagonal line. Cut along the diagonal line and press the seams toward the red.

Make 4.

2. Using matching red and tan fabrics, sew a red print 2" x 2¼" rectangle to a tan print 2" x 2¼" rectangle along the 2" edges. Press toward the red. Make four of these units.

Make 4.

3. Sew a unit from step 2 to each side of a 2" x 2" tan square as shown. Press toward the red.

4. Sew a half-square-triangle unit to each side of a unit from step 2 as shown. Press away from the red. Make two.

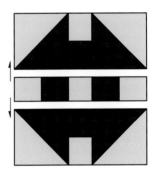

Make 2.

5. Sew the units together as shown to complete the block. Press. Repeat to make 20 blocks.

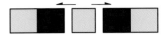

Make 20.

Assembling the Quilt Top

1. Referring to the quilt diagram, lay out your blocks in five rows of four blocks each with 2½" x 9" sashing strips between. Make sure that all the sashing pieces are oriented correctly if using a directional fabric.

2. Sew the blocks and sashing strips together into rows. Then sew the remaining sashing strips and 2½" cornerstones into rows. Press the seams toward the sashing strips.

3. Sew the rows together. Press toward the sashing rows.

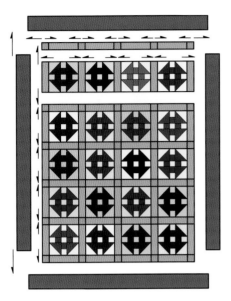

4. For the border, sew the six 4½"-wide strips together end to end with a diagonal seam to create one long piece. Carefully measure through the center of the quilt from top to bottom. Cut two strips from the long border strip to this length. Sew these strips to the left and right sides of the quilt top. Press toward the borders.

5. Measure through the center of the quilt from side to side, including the borders just added. Cut two strips from the remainder of the long border strip to this length. Sew the border strips to the top and bottom of the quilt top. Press toward the borders.

6. Your top is ready to quilt and bind. Refer to "Finishing the Quilt" on page 81 and savor your accomplishment!

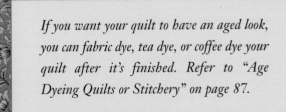

If you want your quilt to have an aged look, you can fabric dye, tea dye, or coffee dye your quilt after it's finished. Refer to "Age Dyeing Quilts or Stitchery" on page 87.

Autumn Bounty Table Mat

Wool appliqué by Rozan Meacham

Fall is Rozan's favorite time of the year, with the crisp smell of apples in the air. Autumn is also rich with the hues of fall colors in pumpkins, gourds, and cornstalks. This project is a reminder of childhood, when a walk through the harvest field included collecting a basket full of leaves and pumpkins. Rozan collects funky primitive crows that make her laugh, so it was natural to include one of them in this gathering basket full of fall treasures.

FINISHED SIZE: 17" x 22"

Materials

Wool yardage amounts are generously estimated and based on 54"-wide fabric. Wash new wool before using.

- ½ yard of tan wool for background and hexagons
- ½ yard of camel wool for backing
- 12" x 12" piece of dark green wool for outer oak leaves
- 8" x 12" piece of brown herringbone wool for field basket
- 5" x 10" piece of black wool for crow body
- 7" x 7" piece of gold wool for gourd and crow beak
- 7" x 7" piece of orange wool for pumpkin
- 6" x 6" piece of light green wool for oak leaves, apple leaf, and pear stem
- 6" x 6" piece of medium green wool for oak leaves and pumpkin stem
- 5" x 5" piece of brown wool for acorn bottoms, apple stem, and gourd stem
- 4" x 4" piece of greenish gold wool for pear
- 3" x 5" piece of charcoal wool for crow wing and eye
- 3" x 3" piece of red wool for apple
- 3" x 3" piece of light brown wool for acorn caps
- Freezer paper

- Fine-point, black permanent marking pen
- 10" x 12" piece of tulle or netting
- Chalk marking pencil
- 505 Spray and Fix basting spray
- Size 22 chenille needle *OR* size 8 embroidery needle
- 1 skein *each* of embroidery floss in 3 different greens for leaves
- 1 skein *each* of brown, gold, and orange embroidery floss for appliqués
- 2 skeins of tan embroidery floss for background
- 1 skein of red embroidery floss for apple and French knots for berries
- 1 skein of dark brown embroidery floss for branches

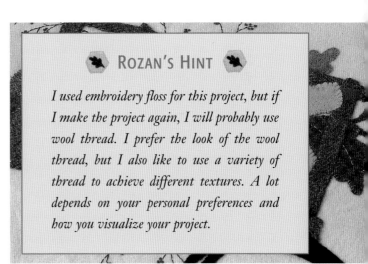

🍂 ROZAN'S HINT 🍂

I used embroidery floss for this project, but if I make the project again, I will probably use wool thread. I prefer the look of the wool thread, but I also like to use a variety of thread to achieve different textures. A lot depends on your personal preferences and how you visualize your project.

Cutting

Trace the pattern pieces on pages 65 and 66 onto freezer paper and cut out on the line. Do not add seam allowances to wool appliqué pieces. Iron the freezer-paper pattern onto the wool and cut out the shapes. If a pattern piece is reversed, just flip the wool shape over; you can use either side of the wool.

From the tan wool and the camel wool, cut from _each_:
- 1 oval
- 21 hexagons

From the light green wool, cut:
- 2 oak leaves
- 1 apple leaf
- 1 pear stem

From the brown herringbone wool, cut:
- 1 basket handle
- 1 basket bottom
- 2 basket sides

From the gold wool, cut:
- 1 gourd
- 1 crow beak

From the orange wool, cut:
- 1 pumpkin

From the black wool, cut:
- 1 crow body

From the charcoal wool, cut:
- 1 crow wing
- 1 crow eye

From the brown wool, cut:
- 5 acorn bottoms
- 1 apple stem
- 1 gourd stem

From the greenish gold tweed wool, cut:
- 1 pear

From the medium green wool, cut:
- 3 oak leaves
- 1 pumpkin stem

From the dark green wool, cut:
- 21 outer oak leaves

From the red wool, cut:
- 1 apple

From the light brown wool, cut:
- 5 acorn caps

Appliquéing the Design

Refer to "Basic Steps for Wool Appliqué" on page 86.

1. For placement, use the pattern on page 66 as a guide. Arrange all the pieces on the tan oval background. Then spray each piece with the basting spray.

2. Use two strands of embroidery floss and whipstitch the pumpkin down. Stitch the handle of the basket about halfway across. Stitch the pumpkin stem.

3. Whipstitch the horizontal basket handle over the oak leaf. Stitch the right side of the gourd and the stem of the gourd. Then stitch the right basket handle.

4. Stitch the basket bottom.

5. Whipstitch the two oak leaves on the left side of the basket. Stitch the left basket handle and the three acorns in the lower-left corner.

6. Whipstitch the pear, the pear stem, the apple, the apple stem, and the apple leaf.

7. Whipstitch the three oak leaves and two acorns in the upper right.

8. Stitch the crow body on top of the basket and stitch the crow beak. Stitch the crow wing.

9. Attach the eye to the crow with a French knot.

10. Trace the pattern for the branches and berries on the tulle or netting with a permanent marking pen. Place the tulle or netting on the wool appliquéd piece and trace over your pattern with the marking pen to mark the pattern for the branches and berries.

11. Backstitch the branches with one strand of dark brown floss. Using one strand of red floss, stitch the berries with a French knot.

12. Whipstitch an outer oak leaf on each of the 21 tan hexagon pieces.

13. Spray the wrong side of the camel oval backing with 505 Spray and Fix basting spray. Place the appliquéd piece on top of the backing, trimming the backing to fit if needed. Blanket stitch the two pieces together.

14. Spray the hexagon camel backing pieces with basting spray and place the hexagons with the leaf on top. Blanket stitch around each piece.

15. Arrange the hexagon pieces around the large oval before stitching them together. Pin them in place.

16. Unpin a hexagon, and with the leaf side facing down on the large oval, whipstitch it to the large oval. Add the next hexagon in the same way, and then whipstitch them together at the sides. Continue until all the hexagons are attached.

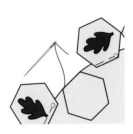

Whipstitch.   Stitch together.

17. Remember to place a label on the back. Have fun decorating with your table mat!

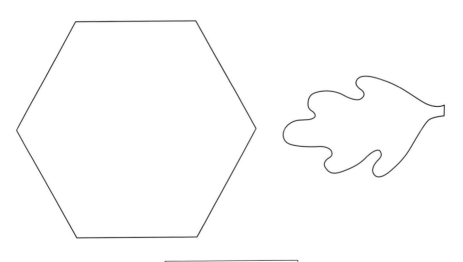

These patterns are full-size.
Cut 42 hexagons
and 21 leaves.

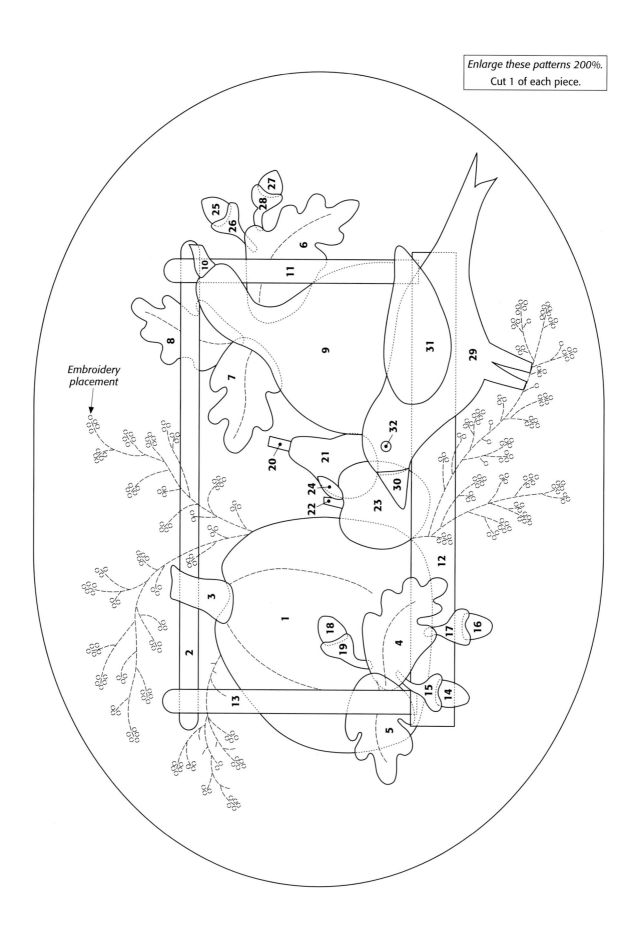

Enlarge these patterns 200%.
Cut 1 of each piece.

Embroidery placement

Poppies Wall Hanging

Wool appliqué by Rozan Meacham

B right gold and red poppies bloom in the early days of summer in eastern Washington where Rozan lives. She loves the colors of red and orange scattered around her front garden, greeting her as she walks up the sidewalk. Since poppies are tricky to cut and use in arrangements, she designed this bowl of poppies to enjoy all year long.

FINISHED SIZE: 16" x 20"

Materials

Wool yardage amounts are generously estimated and based on 54"-wide fabric. Wash new wool before using.

- 20" x 24" piece of black herringbone wool for background
- 18" x 18" piece of green wool or wool army blanket for stems, leaves, and poppy pods
- 10" x 10" piece of medium orange wool for poppies
- 10" x 10" piece of dark orange wool for poppies
- 8" x 12" piece of black wool for bowl and poppy pod centers
- 8" x 8" piece of gold wool for poppy centers and star
- Wool or cotton thread, or embroidery floss, to match fabrics
- Size 22 chenille needle OR size 8 embroidery needle
- Freezer paper
- Chalk marking pencil
- Fine-point, black permanent marking pen
- 505 Spray and Fix basting spray
- 16" x 20" black frame

Cutting

Enlarge the pattern pieces on page 69 and trace them onto freezer paper; cut out on the line. Do not add seam allowances to the wool appliqué pieces. Iron the freezer-paper pattern onto the wool and cut out the shapes.

From the black wool, cut:
- 1 bowl
- 3 poppy pod centers

From the green wool, cut:
- 4 leaves
- 5 stems
- 3 poppy pods

From the medium orange wool, cut:
- 3 poppies

From the dark orange wool, cut:
- 2 poppies

From the gold wool, cut:
- 5 poppy centers
- 1 star

Appliquéing the Design

Refer to "Basic Steps for Wool Appliqué" on page 86.

1. Use the pattern below as a placement guide. Arrange the pieces on the background, placing the black bowl on the background first.

2. Place the stems, inserting them just under the top of the bowl. Add the poppy pods and the leaves. When satisfied with the arrangement, spray each piece with the basting spray.

3. Using one strand of thread, whipstitch each wool piece to the background.

4. Place the poppies on the stems and whipstitch

them with matching thread. Add the poppy centers and whipstitch them with matching thread.

5. Place the black centers on the poppy pods and whipstitch them with matching thread.

6. Place the star on the bowl; whipstitch it with matching thread.

7. Rozan used a frame purchased at a craft store and had the wall hanging stretched and framed. She chose not to use glass in the frame so that the textures of the wool are exposed. You may also choose to frame the project yourself.

8. Make a label and attach it to the back.

Enlarge patterns 275%.
Cut 1 of each piece.

Pincushions are fun to make and collect. Over the years Rozan has collected primitive pincushions, and many friends give them to her for gifts. This design incorporates both wool appliqué and wool needle felting. It's a fast and easy project to make. Give it to a friend who sews or someone who just needs a pick-me-up. These cheerful yellow flowers in a bright red bowl will put a smile on anyone's face.

FINISHED SIZE: 6" diameter

Materials

Materials are based on ½-ounce balls of wool roving.

- 8" x 8" piece of gold tweed wool for pincushion
- 8" x 8" piece of brown plaid wool for backing
- 3" x 6" piece of red wool for bowl
- 2" x 3" piece of green wool for stems
- 1 ball of yellow wool roving for flowers and star
- 1 ball of orange wool roving for flower centers
- 1 ball of red wool roving for star center
- Felting needle and foam pad
- Embroidery needle
- 1 skein of black or brown embroidery floss
- 1 skein of green embroidery floss
- 1 skein of red embroidery floss
- Template plastic or freezer paper
- Polyester or wool stuffing
- Tapestry needle
- Fine-tip black permanent marking pen
- Chalk marking pencil

Cutting

Make templates from freezer paper or template plastic, using the pattern on page 72, including the circle for the backing and background. Add a ¼" seam allowance to the background and the backing as you cut them out.

From the gold tweed wool, cut:
- 1 pincushion background piece

From the red wool, cut:
- 1 bowl

From the green wool, cut:
- 3 flower stems

From the brown plaid wool, cut:
- 1 pincushion backing

Appliqué, Needle Felting, and Embroidery

1. Position the red bowl and green flower stems on the gold tweed background, spraying the backs with adhesive spray. Whipstitch the pieces in place with matching embroidery floss.

2. Trace the flower template onto the background using a black marking pen or chalk marker. Refer to "Needle Felting" on page 93 and place your foam on a mat. Place a small, thin piece of yellow roving inside the flower design, and gently stab with your felting needle to hold the wool in place. Using the tapestry needle, move the roving as you're stabbing it to form the flower.

   Repeated stabbing felts the flower. To get a smooth surface without hardening the center, use shallow stabs. Shaping is created by the depth and direction of the stabs. Add layers of yellow roving until you have the shape and density you want.

3. Roll a small amount of orange wool roving into a ball; felt it into the center of the flower. The more you stab the smaller it will become. Repeat steps 2 and 3 to make the other flowers.

4. Trace the star onto the bowl. Position the wool roving inside the design and felt the star and the center of the star.

5. Draw the vines onto the gold tweed background. Using two or three strands of brown or black embroidery floss, backstitch the vines.

6. Using the green floss, embroider stems on the two shorter flowers with a backstitch.

Finishing

1. Sew the pincushion and backing right sides together, using a ¼" seam allowance and leaving 2" unsewn for turning. Turn the pincushion right side out and stuff. Rozan used wool roving to stuff the pincushion, but you can use polyester stuffing or make an inside lining out of muslin and fill it with sand. Sew the opening shut with a whipstitch.

2. Make a label for your pincushion and sew it to the bottom.

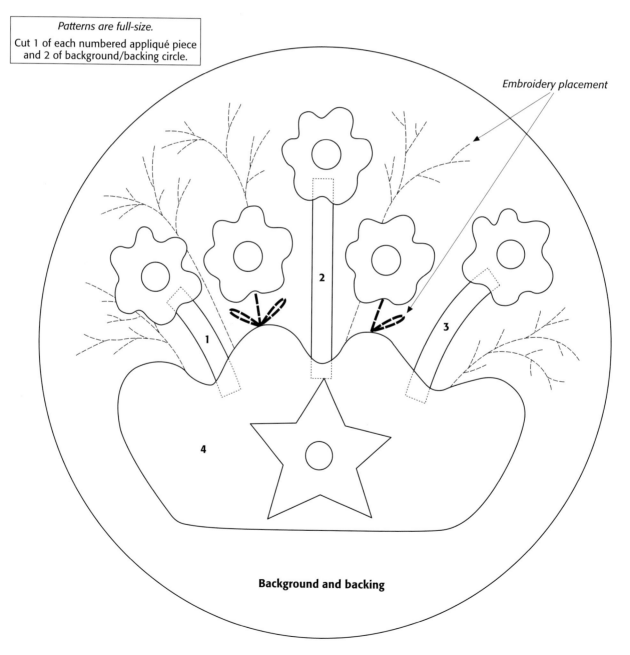

Patterns are full-size.
Cut 1 of each numbered appliqué piece and 2 of background/backing circle.

Embroidery placement

Background and backing

Things I Like Best about Fall Quilt

Like Rozan, Terry's favorite season is fall. When you can smell the apple cider simmering on the wood stove and hear the leaves rustling in the wind, you know fall is upon you. Terry designed this delightful table topper quilt to bring the cozy feeling of autumn into your home. The homespun plaids and primitive stichery will remind you of everything you love about the season.

Materials

All yardages are based on 42"-wide fabric.

- Assorted medium and dark homespun plaid scraps to total ½ yard for square patches
- ⅜ yard of brown print for outer border
- ¼ yard of muslin or other light fabric for inner border
- ⅜ yard of fabric for binding *OR* ½ yard for bias binding
- ⅞ yard of fabric for backing
- 29" x 29" piece of cotton batting
- Brown Pigma pen, size .005, *OR* water-soluble marker
- Embroidery floss in colors of your choice for stitching
- Embroidery needle
- Embroidery hoop
- Light box (optional)

Cutting

From the plaid scraps, cut:
- 100 squares, 2" x 2"

From the muslin, cut:
- 2 strips, 2" x 15½"
- 2 strips, 2" x 18½"

From the brown print, cut:
- 2 strips, 2½" x 18½"
- 2 strips, 2½" x 22½"

Assembling the Quilt Top

1. Sew ten 2" squares into a row. Make 10 rows. Press the seams in opposite directions from row to row.

2. Sew the rows together, pressing the seams in one direction.

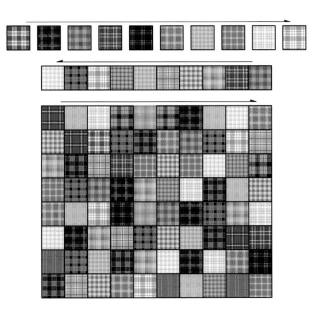

3. Sew the two 2" x 15½" muslin strips to the left and right sides of the quilt center. Sew the 2" x 18½" muslin strips to the top and bottom of the quilt.

4. Sew the two 2½" x 18½" brown print strips to the left and right sides of the quilt. Sew the two 2½" x 22½" outer-border strips to the top and bottom.

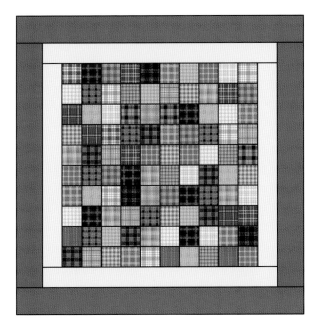

5. Trace the embroidery patterns from page 76 onto the inner border, using the Pigma pen and a light box. Randomly place the words where you'd like them on the fabric. You can also add your own words to personalize your table topper. Place the quilt in an embroidery hoop and stitch the designs using a backstitch and two strands of embroidery floss.

Finishing

1. Layer and baste the quilt top with batting and backing.

2. Quilt by hand or machine. Terry finished her table topper quilt by machine quilting in a diagonal across only the center. This gives the piece interesting dimension and an old-fashioned look. Stitch straight lines or another simple design in the borders.

3. Bind the quilt using straight-grain or bias-cut binding strips. A plaid cut on the bias is a nice complement to the plaids in the center. See "Binding" on page 81.

   If you want a more antique look, dye your table topper after binding. Refer to "Age Dyeing Quilts or Stitchery" on page 87.

clear moon frost soon   Turkey

gather pumpkins   maple leaves

hayrides   crackling fire

apple cider   Patterns are full-size.   friends

gourds   golden wheat fields

Giving Thanks   Harvest moon

Bittersweet   rustling Leaves

harvest herbs   Scarecrows

rake leaves

QUILTMAKING

In this section we cover the basics of quilt-making. Use it as a guide when making any of the quilt projects in this book.

Fabric

When choosing fabric for quilt projects, look for high-quality, 100% cotton. This ensures that the time you spend making your quilt will be reflected in its durability and longevity. Cotton fabric is easily manipulated and lightweight.

All of the projects in this book use 42"-wide fabric. Yardages are calculated on having 40" of useable width after prewashing your fabric.

PREWASHING

Terry generally doesn't prewash fabrics. She pieces her quilts with unwashed fabrics, assembles them with cotton batting, quilts them, and then gently washes them. She then dries them in the dryer; this gives the quilts a puckered, softly aged vintage look that she loves.

Some dark fabrics pose the risk of bleeding, so test fabrics to see if they are colorfast. Place a swatch of the fabric in a bowl of very warm water with a drop of mild detergent for several minutes. Remove the swatch and press it between a few layers of white paper towels. If there's any color residue on the paper towels, use a different fabric.

If you prefer to prewash your fabrics, use warm water with a mild detergent. Dry the fabric in a clothes dryer until it's barely damp, and then iron the remaining wrinkles from the fabric. Prewashing helps remove any excess dye left in the fabric.

COLOR SCHEMES AND PRINTS

Each project in the book provides a color palette to work with. To ensure that you're pleased with the outcome, take some time to study whether the colors are low contrast or highly defined. Also consider the size, scale, and variety of the prints you choose. Spending a little extra time when choosing your fabrics will help make sure you're happy with the result.

Supplies

Having these basic supplies at hand will make your quilting trouble free.

Acrylic ruler. Clear, hard-plastic rulers come in a variety of shapes and sizes. Rozan's favorite is the 6" x 24" ruler made by Omnigrid. Terry likes the 6½" x 24½" ruler made by Creative Grids. Either size is perfect for cutting strips. A square ruler, either 6½" x 6½" or 9½" x 9½", is helpful for squaring up blocks and fabric, and for cutting smaller pieces.

Rotary cutter and mat. A rotary cutter and mat are must-have items. These tools will make your life much simpler.

Iron. Having an iron with a smooth, nonstick surface ensures accurate pressing. Also, a lightweight iron is easier on your wrists than a heavier one.

Sewing machine. You'll need a machine with a nice straight stitch for piecing, and a walking foot and darning foot if you're going to machine quilt.

Machine needles. Using a new needle with a new project is always a good idea. For machine piecing, size 12/80 needles work well. When machine quilting, use a larger needle, size 14/90.

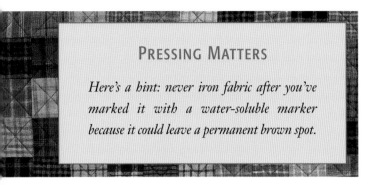

PRESSING MATTERS

Here's a hint: never iron fabric after you've marked it with a water-soluble marker because it could leave a permanent brown spot.

Thread. Always use a high-quality, all-purpose cotton thread.

Pins. Choose long, fine silk pins. They slide effortlessly through fabrics. Terry likes the glass-headed pins that come in two colors; use the white pins on dark fabric and the navy pins on light fabric.

Scissors. Good scissors will give you good cuts. Use only your best scissors to cut fabric. Keep a second pair of craft scissors to cut paper, fusible web, and template plastic.

Seam ripper. Keep this tool right next to you when sewing. The sharper it is, the faster the "unsewing" will go.

Template plastic. Use clear or frosted plastic to make templates. You can find it at your local quilt store.

Water-soluble markers. Use a fine-tipped fabric marker. Test it on a scrap of fabric before marking your quilt to ensure that the marks are easily removed.

Rotary Cutting

Rotary cutting is fast and accurate. When rotary cutting, a standard ¼" seam allowance is included in the measurements. If you are new to rotary cutting, here's a great book to learn more: *The*

Quilter's Quick Reference Guide by Candace Eisner Strick (Martingale & Company, 2004).

Before you rotary cut, press all your fabrics. Creases and wrinkles make cutting inaccurate. Ironing helps the fabric lie flat for cutting. Cut all pieces on the straight of the grain unless otherwise instructed.

1. Fold your fabric in half with the selvages together. Align the crosswise and lengthwise grain as best you can. Lay your fabric on the cutting mat with the folded edge closest to you, as straight as possible. Place a square ruler along the folded edge of the fabric. Line up your long, straight acrylic ruler on the left-hand side of the fabric, covering just the uneven raw edges of the fabric as shown.

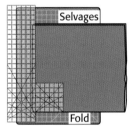

2. Remove the square ruler and cut along the right edge of the long ruler, rolling the rotary cutter away from you. Throw away this scrap. If you're left-handed, simply reverse this procedure.

3. To cut strips from the fabric, align the freshly cut edge of the fabric with the correct width on the acrylic ruler. Always cut away from you,

and be sure to close the rotary-cutter blade whenever you lay the tool down.

4. To cut squares or rectangles, cut strips in the required width. Trim the selvage ends of the strips and align the left edge of the strips with the correct ruler markings. Cut squares or rectangles until you have the number needed.

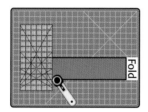

Piecing

Machine piecing enables us to create family heirlooms in record time. Set your machine to sew about 12 to 15 stitches per inch. When piecing, use a ¼" seam allowance for all sewing. Your machine may have a foot that measures ¼" from the center of the needle position to the side of the foot. This ¼" foot is used by many quilters—we love it! It keeps you on the straight and narrow, ensuring that seams are a consistent ¼".

If you don't have this handy ¼" foot, keep your seams straight by placing a piece of tape or a magnetic seam guide on your machine ¼" from the needle.

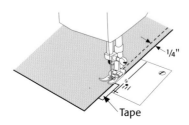

Pressing

To ensure that your pieced blocks fit together accurately, carefully press each seam after sewing. Terry prefers a hot, dry iron for best results. Usually you'll press toward the darker fabric, but sometimes that isn't possible. Lay your patchwork on the ironing board with the darker side (or the side you're pressing toward) on top. Give this seam a quick press; fold back the top piece and press the seam flat.

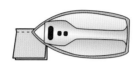 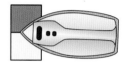

Assembling the Quilt Top

Putting the quilt top together is one of the most rewarding stages in quilting. At this point you get to sew the blocks together and add borders to frame your blocks.

It's a great idea to take the time to square up all of your blocks to the appropriate size. This step will help ensure that the quilt will go together smoothly and quickly. If you have blocks that are too large, trim them down. You may find that there are a few blocks that are too small. Check the seam allowance to make sure you used an accurate ¼".

To make sure you'll be satisfied with the finished results, arrange your quilt on a design wall or on the floor before you sew it together. It's much easier to change your color arrangement before you sew your quilt top together.

Once you begin sewing the blocks together, alternate your pressing direction from row to row so that the seams will butt together when you sew the rows together.

ADDING BORDERS

Most of Terry's quilts have butted borders. This technique is simple and is appropriate for the look of a vintage quilt. To make butted borders, follow these steps.

1. Carefully measure through the center of the quilt from top to bottom. Cut two strips from the border fabric to this length (piece the border strips as needed). Find the midpoint in both your border and quilt by folding them in half and pinning the center. Pin the borders on the left and right sides of your quilt, matching the midpoint and ends. Using a ¼" seam allowance, sew these strips to the quilt. Press toward the borders.

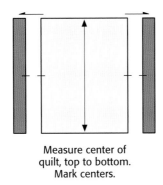

Measure center of
quilt, top to bottom.
Mark centers.

2. Measure through the center of the quilt from side to side, including the borders that you just added. Cut two strips from the border fabric to the length you just measured. Find the midpoint in both the quilt top and the borders. Pin your border strips to the top and bottom of the quilt top and sew. Press toward the borders Repeat steps 1 and 2 for any additional borders.

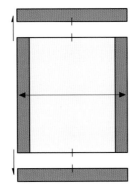

Mark centers.
Measure center of quilt, side to
side, including border strips.

⬟ TERRY'S HINT ⬟

Make sure you lay your quilt out on a hard, flat surface when you're measuring to obtain the most precise measurement. Remember that your quilt will sometimes "grow" or stretch along the outside edges. That's why it's important to measure through the center. Then ease the quilt to fit the borders.

BORDERS WITH CORNER SQUARES

Making borders with corner squares is easier than it looks. Just give it a try and you'll love the results.

1. Measure the length and width of your quilt top through the center.

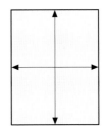

Measure center of quilt top
in both directions.

2. Cut the four borders to these measurements. Mark the midpoint of the border strips and the quilt by folding the fabric in half and pinning it. Sew the left and right side borders onto the quilt.

3. Cut four corner squares the same width as your borders. Sew the corner squares onto the ends of the remaining two borders. Press the seams toward the border strips. Find the

midpoints and pin the borders to the quilt top. Sew and press the seams toward the borders.

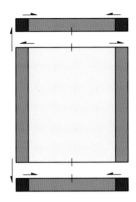

Finishing the Quilt

This section covers how to get the look and feel of a vintage quilt through your choice of batting, backing, and quilting.

BATTING

The two most common types of batting are 100% cotton and a polyester-cotton blend. We prefer 100%-cotton batting because it gives the most authentic vintage look. With this batting, your quilt will have a soft, puckered look due to the shrinkage of the batting and the fabric after you gently wash it. If you don't like the vintage look, use a polyester-cotton blend batting. With both types of batting, cut it 3" to 4" larger than the quilt top on all sides.

BACKING

When selecting a backing for your quilt, try to choose a fabric that coordinates with the quilt top. To keep fabrics consistent, use 100% cotton. Cut the backing 3" to 4" larger than the quilt top on all sides.

QUILTING

The most common methods of quilting are hand quilting, machine quilting, and long-arm machine quilting.

Hand quilting. Terry reserves hand quilting for her best quilts because it is labor intensive. If you'd like to try hand quilting, start with a small project first. A great book to reference is *Loving Stitches, Revised Edition* by Jeana Kimball (Martingale & Comp-any, 2003). If you want to hand quilt but don't have the time, ask the folks at your local quilt store if they know anyone who hand quilts. Most hand quilters charge by the yard of thread.

Machine quilting. Machine quilting at home is a great way to quilt the lap-sized quilts in this book. It's more difficult to machine quilt at home on larger quilts such as queen or king sizes.

Decide on the overall quilting pattern before you begin. Make a sketch of the pattern on paper. If the design is complex, mark your quilt first. Most of the quilts in this book lend themselves well to straight-line quilting, outline quilting the blocks, or free-motion quilting in a random pattern. All of these are easy to do with your home machine. A great book to reference on machine quilting is *Machine Quilting Made Easy!* by Maurine Noble (Martingale & Company, 1994). You can also ask at your local quilt store for tips and classes on machine quilting.

Long-arm machine quilting. Many individuals do machine quilting out of their own home or small business on a long-arm machine. Ask friends and inquire at your local quilt shop for references.

BINDING

Terry uses double-fold binding on her quilts because it's a nice, strong binding that will wear well, and it fits with the vintage style. Use 100%-cotton fabric that coordinates with the quilt top for the binding.

1. Measure around the outside of your quilt, and then add an extra 10" for seams. Cut enough 2¼"-wide strips from your fabric, either on the bias or across the width of the fabric, to

add up to the length needed. Plaids look nice cut on the bias, and you'll need to cut bias strips for curved edges.

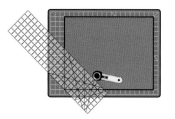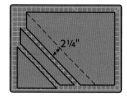

2. Sew the strips together with diagonal seams to create a continuous strip. Trim the seams to ¼" and press the seams open. Fold this strip in half, with wrong sides together, and press.

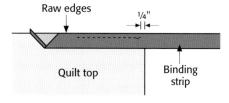

3. To attach the binding, start in the middle of the quilt on any side. Align the binding with the raw edges of the quilt. Terry pins the binding onto the quilt before sewing because it gives her better control. Using a ¼" seam allowance, begin sewing and stop ¼" from the first corner; backstitch.

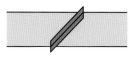

Raw edges   ¼"

Quilt top   Binding strip

4. Remove the quilt from your sewing machine. Fold the binding up, creating a 45° angle at the corner, and back down over itself, lining the binding up to the next side of the quilt. Be sure to square up the binding with the corner of the quilt and pin it in place.

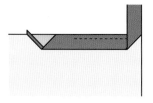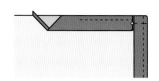

5. Using a ¼" seam, start sewing down the second side of the quilt. Stop when you're ¼" from the next corner and backstitch. Remove your quilt and repeat step 4. Continue around the quilt in this manner.

6. Sew to where you started. Cut your binding on an angle, leaving an extra inch to tuck inside the already-sewn binding. Finish stitching the binding down.

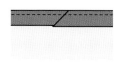

7. Fold the creased edge of the binding to the back of the quilt so that it encloses the raw edges of the quilt and covers the line of stitching. Take care to create mitered corners on both sides of your quilt and pin them in place. Hand sew the binding with a blind stitch, using a thread color that matches the binding.

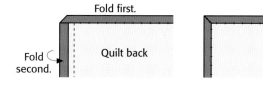

Fold first.

Fold second.   Quilt back

Hand Appliqué: Needle-Turn Method

Of all the ways that quilters can do hand appliqué, Rozan prefers the needle-turn appliqué method. Needle-turn appliqué is a time-honored and time-efficient method of hand appliqué. As the name implies, you use the needle shank and point to turn under the raw edges of your appliqué piece as you stitch them to the background. The seam allowance is narrow, about ⅛", so your appliqué piece will lie flat. The narrow seam also makes it easier to go around corners and make smooth curves. There are many books on appliqué in your local quilt shop with which you can learn other methods. If you prefer another method, please use what is most comfortable for you.

TEMPLATES

Rozan uses freezer paper for making templates, but you can also use template plastic.

1. Using a black marking pen, copy your pattern onto the dull, paper side of freezer paper or onto template plastic. When you cut out your pattern piece, cut to the inside of your mark; otherwise your pattern will be larger than it should be. Do not add a seam allowance.

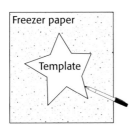

Freezer paper

Template

2. Iron the freezer paper onto the right side of the cotton fabric and trace around it with a permanent ultra-fine-tip black marking pen. If using template plastic, trace around the template onto the right side of the fabric. Using the black marking pen forces you to preserve the original design line because you must turn the marked line under when you stitch. On dark fabrics, use a sharp chalk marking pencil.

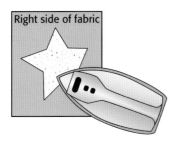

Right side of fabric

3. Cut out your appliqué pieces, adding a ¼" seam allowance. This will be trimmed to ⅛" later when appliquéing the piece to the background.

APPLIQUÉ STITCH

1. Rozan uses the product Roxanne's Glue-Baste-It for temporarily holding appliqué pieces in position on a background, but you can baste them with thread or use appliqué pins. Refer to the pattern for placement. Place the appliqués on the background first to make sure the placement is right, and then gently lift them to glue them in place. Rozan likes to place all her pieces on the background at one time and then appliqué them. Place them one at a time if you prefer.

2. Use a length of thread 12" to 18" long that matches the color of your appliqué piece; thread it through an appliqué or straw needle and tie a knot in one end. Straw needles are long, thin needles that work well for appliqué. Rozan uses a size 10 straw needle.

3. The appliqué stitch is done right to left (left to right if you're left-handed). Begin on a straight edge of the appliqué piece, and trim the seam allowance to ⅛" for a couple of inches. Turn a small section of the edge under. Hold this edge with the thumb of your left hand as you bring the needle up through the fold and then into the background fabric just in front of where you came out of the appliqué piece. Keeping the stitches very small and

close together (no more than ⅛" apart), continue trimming and stitching around your appliqué. Pull the stitches tight but not to the point of making the fabric pucker.

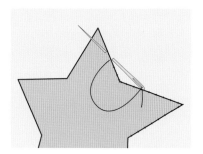

4. To end your stitching, insert the needle under your appliqué piece and into the background fabric to the wrong side. Make a couple of tiny stitches in the background and bring the needle back up through one of the stitches. To make a knot, loop the thread around the needle two times, insert the needle into the background fabric (between the background and appliqué piece), and travel about ½". Bring the needle back out and tug gently to pop the knot through the background fabric. Clip your thread.

POINTS AND CURVES

To create sharp outer points, stitch up to the point of the drawn line and take a tiny stitch to anchor the point. You now have a flap of fabric sticking out at the point. Trim the seam allowance of the downward seam to ⅛". Turn the point under and then the seam, and continue stitching.

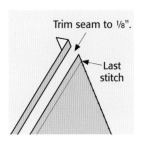
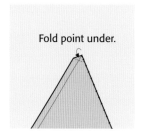

To stitch an inside point, take tiny stitches before you get to the point and clip to the inner point. Don't cut past the drawn line. Turn under the edge to the point. Taking tiny stitches, stitch down to the point. You can use a glue stick to help hold the seam allowance under—get a tiny amount of glue on the tip of your needle and slip it under the seam allowance. With the needle shank, turn the seam allowance under on the other side of the point. Use tiny stitches through the V shape.

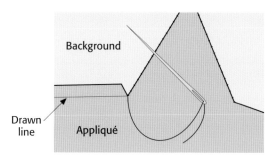

To stitch a curve, such as an S shape, trim your seam allowance to ⅛" and make several clips in the seam allowance, but be careful not to cut past the drawn line. Using your needle shank, turn under the seam allowance and make tiny stitches. You can also use a glue stick on curves. Continue making tiny stitches until you get through the curve.

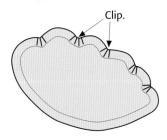

STEMS

Cut stems on the bias of the fabric for greater flexibility and smoother lines. Place your template on the right side of your appliqué fabric, trace around it, and cut it out, adding a ¼" seam allowance. Using the product Roxanne's Glue-Baste-It, put tiny dots of glue down the wrong side of the stem about 1" apart. Position the stem in place. With your appliqué needle and thread, appliqué the stem on one side, trimming the seam allowance to ⅛" as you stitch. You may have to loosen the glue as you stitch down the other side of the stem. If the stem is especially narrow, you may have to pull the appliqué back and trim a little of the seam allowance away before continuing.

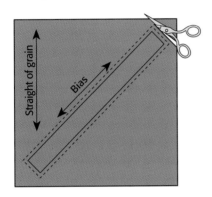

Another way to do a stem if it's fairly straight is to simply cut a bias strip the length needed. Press under the ¼" seam allowances on each side. Place the stem in position and stitch down one side. Open the piece up and trim the seams on each side to ⅛". Fold the appliqué piece back and stitch down the other side. You can also use bias bars, available at quilt shops, to make bias stems. The instructions on how to make the bias stems are included with the bias bars.

CIRCLES

Rozan likes to do circles the old-fashioned way—just needle-turn appliqué around the circle. You'll end up with circles that are not perfect, but the ones found in nature aren't either.

If you prefer to use templates to create more perfect circles, use card stock or heat-resistant template plastic such as Templar to make circle templates. Trace the circles onto the wrong side of the fabric and cut them out, adding a ¼" seam allowance. Using a needle, make a running stitch in your seam allowance. Place the plastic or cardboard template on the wrong side of your fabric and pull it around the template. Steam the circle

with an iron and then stitch it down, using small appliqué stitches so that it won't pucker. Cut an X in the background piece and remove the template. If you use card stock, you may need to remake the template if you have more circles to stitch.

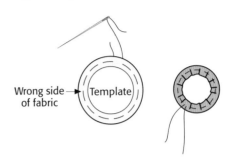

Wool Appliqué

Rozan loves doing wool appliqué. It goes quickly and is easy to do with a few basic stitches. Best of all, there aren't any seam allowances to turn under. The many different types of wool can provide a myriad of textures in your work. Rozan uses a whipstitch for most of her wool appliqué. It's fast and easy and looks a lot like the blanket stitch. She uses the blanket stitch when she needs to finish a raw edge, a backstitch or running stitch for veins and lettering, and a French knot for flowers. Purchase dyed wool or dye your own. (See also "Information about Wool" on page 89.) Wool, silk, prairie cloth, and many other fabrics can be used as backgrounds.

Blanket stitch

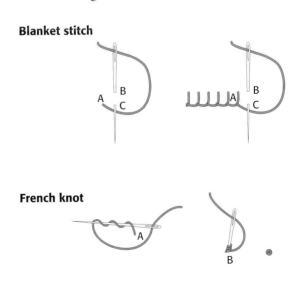

French knot

Running stitch

Whipstitch

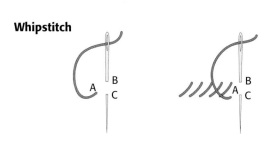

SUPPLIES

The supplies for wool appliqué are minimal and easily found in fabric stores or quilt shops.

Thread. Rozan likes using wool thread, particularly the wool floss by DMC or wool thread by Aurifil. See "Resources" on page 95 for thread sources. You can also use two strands of embroidery floss or size 8 pearl cotton. You can even use one strand of cotton thread for a totally different look.

Needles. Use a needle that has a large enough eye to get the thread through without a lot of work. Rozan uses a size 24 chenille needle; these needles have sharper points than tapestry needles.

Scissors. Fabric scissors work well for cutting out the wool pattern pieces. Make sure the scissors are sharp or you'll get a ragged edge. Rozan prefers a smaller scissor with a sharp point. This gives better control when cutting smaller or detailed wool pieces. She uses embroidery scissors for cutting threads.

Basting spray. 505 Spray and Fix is used as a temporary adhesive for attaching wool pieces to the background. You can move the piece several times after spraying. It washes out, doesn't get hard, and your needle won't get gooey. You can also use a glue stick or simply baste your appliqués.

Freezer paper. Using freezer paper for the pattern templates adds stability to the wool while cutting.

Marker. If you prefer to use template plastic, use a chalk marking pencil to mark around the templates on your wool fabrics.

BASIC STEPS FOR WOOL APPLIQUÉ

1. Cut out the background piece.

2. Trace your appliqué pattern onto the dull, paper side of the freezer paper and cut out just inside the line. Don't add a seam allowance.

3. Iron the freezer-paper pattern onto the wool chosen for the appliqué. Cut out the shape and place it on your background fabric, checking the pattern for placement. If you need a reverse piece cut from wool, cut the shape out and flip the wool piece over; both sides of the wool are the same.

4. Remove the freezer paper and use spray adhesive to place the wool appliqué piece on the background. Continue until all pieces are in place on the background. Rozan stitches her appliqué shapes after they are all positioned. You can place and stitch one piece at a time if you prefer. Just be careful to pay attention to the stitching order.

5. Whipstitch the wool appliqué pieces to the background. Hide your knot under your wool piece. Use a thread color that matches the appliqué if you want it to blend; use a contrasting color if you want your stitches to stand out.

6. Finish your project as directed. If you iron your project, steam it from the wrong side so that you don't create a shine on the wool.

AGE DYEING QUILTS OR STITCHERY

If you want a vintage or aged look, you can "antique" your quilt or stitchery with fabric dye, tea, or coffee. After "antiqueing," dry quilts in the dryer for a soft, crinkled, antique look. With embroidered items, dry them flat or hang from a hanger for all three methods.

Fabric dye. Following the package directions, mix tan dye and water in a spray bottle to resemble weak coffee. (Terry uses Rit brand fabric dye.) Spray your fabric or quilt randomly and let it set up for a few minutes. Then rinse in the washer and dry. If it's a small piece, rinse by hand in the sink.

Tea dye. Make a solution of tea that look like a regular cup of tea—be sure to leave out milk and sugar. You can either submerge your quilt in the tea or pour the solution into a spray bottle and spritz until you get the desired look. Rinse in cool water. Keep in mind that a quilt will be lighter in color when it dries.

Coffee dye. Make a pot of weak coffee (or use instant coffee), and follow the instructions for tea dyeing.

Hand Embroidery

Embroidery is a simple and relaxing art form. Terry always has a project with her when she travels. Begin by tracing the pattern onto your background fabric. A light box is very handy for this, but not essential. Terry uses a brown Pigma pen to make very fine lines. You can also use a water-soluble marker and rinse the piece after it's stitched to remove the marks.

 SUPPLIES IN TERRY'S EMBROIDERY KIT

- Embroidery needle (size 7 is her favorite)
- Embroidery hoop
- Embroidery floss
- Small pair of scissors
- Pigma pen, size .005
- Light box

Embroidery Stitches

For the projects in this book, you'll stitch with one to three strands of embroidery floss using two basic stitches: backstitch and French knot. The French knot is illustrated on page 85.

Backstitch. The backstitch is a quick, basic stitch with a length of ⅛" to ¼". The length of the stitches and the spacing between them can vary depending on the look of the stitchery.

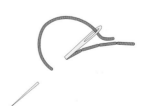

— Primitive Rug Hooking —

ozan enjoys primitive rug hooking immensely. Primitive rug hooking is usually done with wider wool strips than traditional rug hooking, and the designs are simpler, less formal, and often whimsical, with a folk-art look. Wool strips used in primitive rugs are cut ¼" to ⅜" wide.

Rug hooking requires a minimum of tools and supplies. You'll need a hook, a frame, and something to cut wool strips. To start out, you can use a quilting hoop as a frame and use your rotary cutter and ruler to cut strips. There are rug-hooking frames that you can purchase, but many rug hookers like quilting frames and use them exclusively.

Rozan's preferred hook is a Nancy Miller primitive hook, which is shaped like a pencil. She also uses a Moshimer primitive hook; the head is larger so that it makes a bigger hole in the backing for your hook to go through. Try several to see which you prefer. Also, there are many rug-hooking instruction books available in places such as quilt shops. The one Rozan likes to use for teaching is *Purely Primitive* by Pat Cross (Martingale & Company, 2003).

Preparing the Backing

Traditionally, rugs were hooked using burlap feed sacks. Scottish burlap is used today, in addition to monk's cloth and linen. Rozan prefers primitive linen for her backing. It is softer than burlap and easy to work with, but it is more expensive than the other options.

1. Cut your backing to the size stated in the pattern you're using. The backing should generally be a minimum of 4" larger on each side than your pattern when using a rug-hooking frame, or at least 8" larger on each side if you are using a hoop. When cutting, follow a line of thread so that your backing will be on the straight of grain.

2. Serge the edges of the backing or zigzag stitch them on your sewing machine so that they won't fray as you hook your rug.

Transferring the Pattern

The rug-hooking patterns in this book are reduced and will need to be enlarged. You can use a photocopier yourself, take the pattern to a copy shop, or enlarge them by hand following the grid printed behind each pattern. When the design is the correct size, make templates out of plastic or freezer paper.

1. Use a permanent black marking pen and a ruler to mark the dimension of your rug onto the backing fabric. Be sure that you're on the straight of grain when you mark the backing.

2. Using the pattern as a guide, place the templates onto your backing fabric. Trace around the templates with the black marking pen.

Information about Wool

To get the look of a primitive rug, use paisleys, plaids, checks, and herringbones. Your wool can be new or gently used wool from thrift-store clothing. Either way, be sure to wash the wool first as directed below. This not only ensures that it is clean, it also shrinks it a bit and thickens it so that it is the perfect texture for your rug.

To determine the amount of wool you'll need, measure the area to be hooked to determine the surface area, and multiply that number by four. For example, a 3" x 4" rectangle is equal to 12 square inches. Determine square inches by multiplying the width (in this example, 3") by the length (in this example, 4"). Then multiply the total number of square inches by 4. In our example, you would multiply 12 by 4. You need a minimum of 48 square inches of wool. This could be a piece that measures, for example, 4" x 12" or 3" x 16". Always purchase more wool than you need and use the leftovers for other projects.

WASHING WOOL

If you're buying hand-dyed wool, someone has already done the washing for you. If you're purchasing new wool yardage or using 100%-wool garments from a thrift store, you'll need to wash the wool before using it. Wash the wool in your washing machine with a bit of detergent and hot water. Do not use fabric softener. Rinse with cold water; this change in temperature helps with the felting process. Dry the wool in the dryer until damp-dry. Then lay it flat to finish drying. Take garments apart and wash them again to remove the lint and dust from the seam areas.

CUTTING STRIPS

For the projects in this book, you will need strips of wool ¼" wide. Rozan uses a Townsend cutter made especially for cutting strips for rug hooking. You can also use a rotary cutter. To make sure that you cut your wool on the straight of grain, make a snip at one end of the wool and then tear a strip off. Use this as your straight edge.

If you're using a cutting mat and rotary cutter, use the reverse side of your cutting mat to cut your wool strips because the wool will leave some fibers in the mat. Cut strips ¼" wide and 17" to 18" long. If you are using a wool cutter, set it for 8 (¼" wide).

Don't cut all your wool at one time because the strips have a tendency to tangle. Rozan places her cutter near her and cuts additional strips as she needs them.

❀ **ROZAN'S HINT** ❀

Gather strips of the same-color wool in a bundle, tie it with one of the strips, and put the bundle in a plastic bag to keep the strips from tangling.

Hooking the Rug

1. Put the backing into a frame or quilting hoop, making sure that the background is straight and taut.

2. With your left hand, hold a ¼"-wide strip of wool under the hoop. Hold your hook like a pencil in your right hand and push the hook through a hole in the backing fabric.

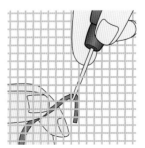

3. Hook the wool strip and pull the short end up to the top. Bring it up about ½"—this is your "tail." (These directions are written for right-handed hooking; if you're left-handed, reverse the process.)

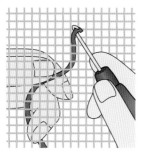

4. Insert the hook into the next hole and with a sweeping motion hook the wool strip that your left hand is keeping straight, and pull it through the hole. Pull the wool up and away from you. The loop should be about ¼" high, roughly the same height as the width of the strip. Carefully remove the hook.

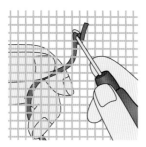

5. For the next loop, insert the hook two to three holes away. You want the loops close enough so that you can't see the backing, but if you hook too closely your rug won't lie flat. The wool strips should cover the area, with the loops just touching. All the loops should be the same height. Continue to hook loops in this manner, with the underneath hand holding the wool strip, and the upper hand using the hook.

Note: *Always hook* inside *the black marked pattern lines or your design will be too large.*

6. Continue hooking until you get to the end of the wool strip; leave a tail about 1" long on top. All strips begin and end on top. The tails will be trimmed off later.

7. To start a new strip of wool or change colors, bring the wool up in the same hole where you ended the previous strip, leaving a ½" to 1" tail on the top, and begin to hook. You don't want all your strips to end in the same spot, so stagger the strips from row to row.

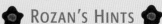

8. Hook around the perimeter of a design before filling in the center area.

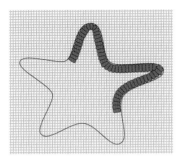

9. Hook the background of the rug last. Hook one or two rows around the outer edges, and then fill in the area, making swirls, S shapes, and echoes of the designs. Trim the tails once they are surrounded by other loops.

Pressing the Rug

When the hooking is done, you must steam the rug. This is a crucial step; it will make your hooked rug lie flat and give it a professional appearance.

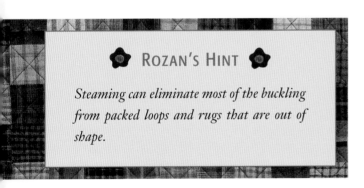

ROZAN'S HINT

Steaming can eliminate most of the buckling from packed loops and rugs that are out of shape.

1. Lay your rug face down on a towel that has been placed on an ironing board.

2. Wet another towel and wring out the excess water. Place the towel over the rug. With the iron on the wool setting, press over the towel. Don't iron back and forth because this might distort the shape. Press thoroughly. When you have finished the first side, turn the rug over

and repeat. When finished, the rug will be slightly damp. Lay it flat to dry.

Finishing the Rug

There are several ways to finish the edges of a rug. The two most common methods are twill binding tape and whipstitching with yarn.

TWILL BINDING TAPE

Using twill binding tape that matches the background of the rug is the most popular method of binding. You can sew binding tape on before or after you hook your rug, but it's easier to apply it before hooking.

Binding may be applied by machine or by hand sewing. If sewing by machine, you must do this before hooking because it's hard to get close to the loops after you hook. If sewing the binding after hooking, it's easier to do this by hand; sew the tape as close to the hooking as possible.

1. Start the binding in the middle of one side. Fold under the starting end about 1" so that the raw edge won't show when the binding is folded over to the back in step 4.

2. Ease the tape around the corners; don't pull too tightly or you won't be able to turn the corners smoothly. Go all the way around and overlap the folded end by ½".

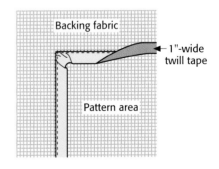

3. Stitch a row or two of stay stitching ¾" from the hooking on the backing either by machine or by hand. Then trim the backing close to this line.

4. After the rug is hooked, fold the binding tape to the back and whipstitch the tape to the back of the rug.

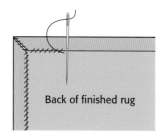

Back of finished rug

WHIPSTITCHING

Whipstitching the edge of the rug with bulky wool yarn is the binding method Rozan prefers; it was used for the rugs in this book. All you need is bulky wool yarn that matches the background.

1. Add a row or two of stay stitching by hand or machine that is 1½" from the hooking. Trim the backing close to the line of stitching.

2. Place the rug on an ironing board with the right side of the rug facing up. Fold the backing allowance in half, pushing it up against the hooked loops. Press with steam, being careful not to burn your fingers. Fold the allowance in half again and press. This will leave about ⅜" of fabric to cover with the wool yarn. Press so that the corners are slightly rounded. You might need to trim a little of the backing away in those areas.

3. Use a thick, bulky yarn that matches the background of your rug. You can also use two strands of four-ply wool. Use a large-eye needle. Leaving a tail of yarn about 2" long, start your whipstitch from the front, moving right to left. You'll be enclosing the yarn tail and folded backing as you stitch. This method results in an evenly stitched edge on the right side of the rug.

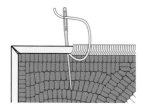

4. To end the stitching, slide the needle underneath the last few stitches that you made. Cut off the leftover yarn.

NEEDLE FELTING

Needle felting is an old art form becoming popular again. It is a waterless felting technique using wool fleece, or roving, and a hand-felting needle. Small barbs on the needle shaft catch and lock the fibers together when the needle is stabbed into the roving. The more you stab, the tighter the fibers will lock together and the firmer the felt will become. See "Resources" on page 95 for suppliers of wool roving and hand-felting needles. You will also need a piece of firm upholstery foam, at least 3" thick, as your work surface. Use a rotary-cutting mat under the foam so that you don't put holes in your table, and follow the steps below.

1. Trace your pattern onto template plastic and trace around it on your wool background with a chalk marking pencil.

2. Place wool roving onto your design. Use a small amount of roving at a time. Start by tacking it in place, using just enough stabs to hold it in place. Then go back and begin stabbing evenly over the surface.

Needle around the shape to hold the edges in place

3. Continue adding small amounts of roving until you get the depth and look that you want. If an area is thin, just add a little roving to it and felt. If the area is too thick, use a tapestry needle to remove some of the roving. You can always pull the entire design off and start over if you don't like the way it looks.

For projects such as the coasters in this book, steam them with an iron after they are complete to make the fibers lie down. This gives the projects a smoother finish.

 TIPS FOR NEEDLE FELTING

- Hold your needle straight up and down. If you twist it or go in at an angle, you can break the needle.
- Bring your needle completely out of the roving before moving to another area.
- The needles are fragile, so use care when poking into the foam. Don't go so deep that you break your needle.
- The needles are sharp, so keep fingers out of the way and use a tapestry needle or tweezers to position the fiber.
- Shaping is created by the depth and directions of the stabs. For a smooth surface without hardening the center, use many shallow stabs.
- Keep picking up your wool background so that it doesn't attach itself to the foam. Trim the excess roving off the back of the design.

RECOMMENDED READING

Beatty, Alice, and Mary Sargent. *Basic Rug Hooking*. Harrisburg, Penn.: Stackpole Books, 1990.

Cross, Pat. *Purely Primitive: Hooked Rugs from Wool, Yarn, and Homespun Scraps*. Woodinville, Wash.: Martingale & Company, 2003.

Lais, Emma Lou, and Barbara Carroll. *Antique Colours for Primitive Rugs: Formulas Using Cushing's Acid Dyes*. Kennebunkport, Maine: W. Cushing and Company, 1996.

Lais, Emma Lou, and Barbara Carroll. *Hooked Rugs: A Primer for Recreating Antique Rugs*. Kennebunkport, Maine: W. Cushing and Company, 1996.

Minick, Polly, and Laurie Simpson: *Folk Art Friends*. Woodinville, Wash.: Martingale & Company, 2003.

Moshimer, Joan. *The Complete Book of Rug Hooking*. New York: Dover Publications, 1989.

Noble, Maurine. *Machine Quilting Made Easy!* Woodinville, Wash.: Martingale & Company, 1994.

Strick, Candace Eisner. *The Quilter's Quick Reference Guide*. Woodinville, Wash.: Martingale & Company, 2004.

Warm up to Wool: Projects to Hook and Stitch. Woodinville, Wash.: Martingale & Company, 2004.

RESOURCES

Blackberry Primitives
1944 High Street
Lincoln, NE 68502
402-421-1361
402-423-8464
www.blackberryprimitives.com
Overdyed and textured wools

The Buggy Barn
28848 Tramm Rd. N
Reardan, WA 99029
509-796-2188
www.buggybarnquilts.com
Wool, fabric, rug-hooking, and quilting supplies

Kindred Spirits
115 Colonial Lane
Kettering, OH 45429
937-435-7758
www.kindredspiritsdesign.com
Rug-hooking supplies, hand-dyed wool, and rotary-cutting systems

Pieceable Dry Goods
5215 W. Clearwater Ave. Suite 106
Kennewick, WA 99336
509-735-6080
www.pieceable.com
Fabric, wool, notions, quilting, Aurifil wool thread, and rug-hooking supplies

Smith and Sage Quilting
Amy Smith
1946 Davison Ave.
Richland, WA 99354
Long-arm machine quilting

Thangles
PO Box 2266
Fond de Lac, WI 54936
877-703-5284
www.thangles.com
Email: thangles@aol.com
Fast and accurate half-square-triangle units

Townsend Industries, Inc.
Box 97
Altoona, IA 50009
877-868-3544
Wool cutter

W. Cushing and Company
PO Box 351
Kennebunkport, ME 04046
800-626-7847
www.wcushing.com
Supplies and dyes for overdyeing wool

ABOUT THE AUTHORS

Rozan Meacham

Rozan Meacham was already an accomplished artist when she took her first quilting class in 1990 from Retta Warehime. She credits her mother, Bettye Kroupa, with her artistic talent. Rozan is a popular teacher at Pieceable Dry Goods in Kennewick, Washington, where she has been sharing her love of quilting since they opened their doors in 1991. She finds that quilting and designing help her relax and unwind after long hours working in the medical field. Her students encouraged her to publish her original designs, and thus "Starry Angel Designs," her pattern company, was born. Rozan also loves to take classes and learn new techniques from other teachers.

Rozan's enthusiasm for collecting treasured antiques, and primitive and American folk art, is evident throughout her home. In nooks and crannies, you'll find treasures of times gone by—handwoven baskets, antique quilts, well-loved bowls and crocks, wooden pineapples, crows with attitude, and angels of every description. Her respect for the women who walked before motivates her to collect these treasured possessions and to add her own voice with her designs that honor the past.

Rozan lives in Pasco, Washington, with her husband, Pat, and her father, Dick Stultz. Rozan and Pat have two lovely daughters, Shannon Johansen and Kerry Meacham, and two greatly treasured grandsons, Jared and Derek, who've been known to say, "Grandma, I think it's time you made me another quilt," or "I've grown too tall and I've outgrown my quilt. Can you make me another one?"

Terry Burkhart

Terry grew up surrounded by sewing. Her mother, Florence, was a wonderful seamstress and her grandmother was a quilter. From a young age she remembers sitting on her mother's lap while her mother carefully pieced her work together, but it wasn't until after Terry grew up and went away to college that she gained an interest in quilting. Her Grandma Minnie sat with her patiently and taught her all about the art form of quilting.

Terry and her family moved from California to Washington State in the late 1970s. They settled in Kennewick and raised four children—John, Sara, Anne, and Betsy. During her initial years in Kennewick, Terry was introduced to Barbara Ward through her local church. They shared a great love for quilting and decided to open a quilt store called Pieceable Dry Goods in 1991. Their quilt store specializes in country style with romantic to primitive looks.

Today Terry's passion in quilting is to study and collect antique quilts. During her free time she enjoys creating patterns that are representative of quilts that could have been found in her grandmother's attic. Terry's husband, Keith, is very supportive of her interest and shares her appreciation of antiques. They are able to enjoy history every day living in their 1899 farmhouse on Keith's family farm. Living on a dry-land wheat farm has been an inspiration for many of Terry's stitchery and quilt designs.